John W. Schaum

Arpeggio Speller

for Piano or Electronic Keyboard

Foreword

The Schaum Arpeggio Speller is a carefully designed workbook that provides the student with a comprehensive knowledge of all major and minor arpeggios. By writing out the notes for the individual arpeggios and also locating them on the keyboard diagrams the student acquires a thorough understanding of their construction. Special drills for writing the correct fingering are part of every lesson. The student is given keyboard assignments in playing the arpeggios in all their inversions in each hand. There are four quiz sections in the book which enable the student to double check him/herself.

Contents

Lesson	page
1. C Major Arpeggio	4
2. G Major Arpeggio	5
3. D Major Arpeggio	6
4. A Major Arpeggio	7
5. E Major Arpeggio	8
6. B Major Arpeggio	9
7. Arpeggio Quiz No. 1	10
8. F Major Arpeggio	11
9. Bb Major Arpeggio	12
10. Eb Major Arpeggio	13
11. Ab Major Arpeggio	14
12. Db Major Arpeggio	15
13. Gb Major Arpeggio	16
14. Arpeggio Quiz No. 2	17
15. A Minor Arpeggio	18
16. E Minor Arpeggio	19
17. B Minor Arpeggio	20
18. F# Minor Arpeggio	21
19. C# Minor Arpeggio	22
20. G# Minor Arpeggio	23
21. Arpeggio Quiz No. 3	24
22. D Minor Arpeggio	25
23. G Minor Arpeggio	26
24. C Minor Arpeggio	27
25. F Minor Arpeggio	28
26. Bb Minor Arpeggio	29
27. Eb Minor Arpeggio	30
28 Arpeggio Quiz No. 4	31

© Copyright 1965 by Schaum Publications, Inc., Mequon, Wisconsin
International Copyright Secured • All Rights Reserved • Printed in U.S.A.
ISBN-13: 978-1-62906-078-1

Progressive Succession of Schaum Workbooks:

Theory Workbook, Level 2
Rhythm Workbook, Level 2
Easy Keyboard Harmony, Book 1 (Level 2)
Scale Speller (Level 2)

Theory Workbook, Level 3
Rhythm Workbook, Level 3
Easy Keyboard Harmony, Book 2 (Level 3)
Arpeggio Speller (Level 3)

Theory Workbook, Level 4
Rhythm Workbook, Level 4
Easy Keyboard Harmony, Book 3 (Level 4)
Interval Speller (Level 4)

Easy Keyboard Harmony, Book 4 (Level 5)
Chord Speller (Level 5)

Easy Keyboard Harmony, Book 5 (Level 6)

Specialty Spellers

- Progressive series provides the foundation needed for study of harmony, musical form and composition
- Systematized worksheets are effective aids to faster music reading
- Valuable supplements for all piano and keyboard methods
- Helpful to string, brass, woodwind and vocal students

Scale Speller (0270) • Level 2
Student writes all major and harmonic minor scales (one octave) for both treble and bass clefs. Scale degree numbers, tetrachords, key signatures and circle of keys are explained. Student also writes in correct fingering and plays each scale at keyboard. Natural and melodic minors are explained.

Arpeggio Speller (0230) • Level 3
Teaches formation of all major and minor arpeggios in root position plus 1st and 2nd inversions, using both treble and bass clefs. Student writes in proper fingering and plays each arpeggio.

Interval Speller (0250) • Level 4
An effective aid to faster music reading through interval recognition. Emphasizes interval analysis and construction. Includes major, minor, perfect, diminished and augmented intervals in all keys. Removable answer page for easy correction.

Chord Speller (0235) • Level 5
Shows how to analyze and construct all basic chords in root position and all inversions. Includes major and minor 6th chords, dominant and diminished 7th chords, altered 7th chords, plus 9th chords. Comprehensive Chord Dictionary.

The Arpeggio Story

A chord is a combination of three or more tones played simultaneously. An ARPEGGIO (ahr-PEJ-oh) is the production of the tones of a chord in rapid succession as in playing the harp. The word arpeggio literally means **harp-like**. See examples 1 and 2 below.

A broken chord is similar to an arpeggio. It is designated by a wavy line preceding it and is performed in **harp-like** style. The notes are played rapidly one after the other, starting with the bottom note. However, the keys are usually held down as they are played. See examples 3 and 4 below. The tones of the arpeggio are not sustained.

How to Use the Book

As the individual lessons are accomplished, all the previous keyboard assignments are to be reviewed daily. Keyboard dexterity is acquired only through diligent repetition. There is a famous anecdote about a musician who was recently appointed to play with the New York Symphony Orchestra. Being a newcomer to the city, he was unfamiliar with the streets and he found himself being late for the first rehearsal. He hailed a taxi cab and asked the driver, "How do I get to Carnegie Hall?" The cabby replied, "Practice, practice, practice." The point of this fable also applies to the amateur musician. He/she may not aspire to perform in Carnegie Hall but just want to play for personal pleasure. Nevertheless, a certain amount of practice is necessary. Piano playing involves physical skills that require drill just as do golf, tennis, swimming and other human performance.

Lesson 1. C Major Arpeggio

Pupil's Name.. Completion Date..

Assignment Date.. Grade or Star..

DIRECTIONS: On the staffs below, write whole notes for the root position and inversions of the C major arpeggio. See chart at bottom of page. The sample is already marked as it should be.

Root Position (Sample) | First Inversion | Second Inversion

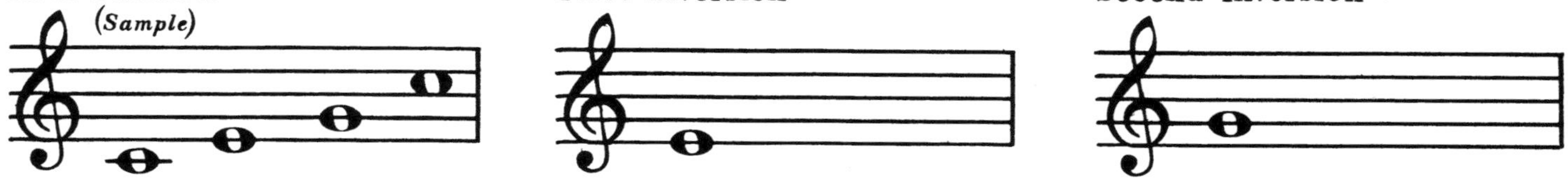

C E G C

(*Write letter names on dotted lines*)

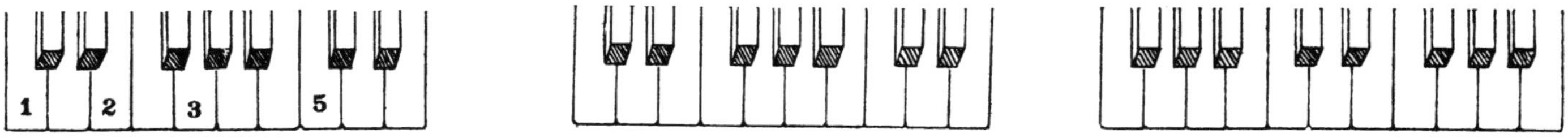

(*Write R.H. finger numbers on keyboard diagrams. See chart below.*)

Root Position | First Inversion | Second Inversion

(*Write letter names on dotted lines*)

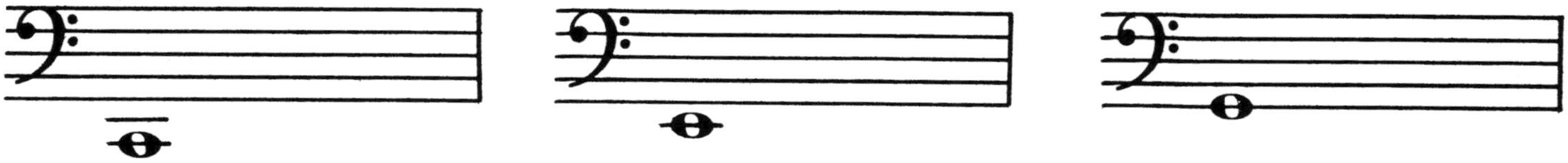

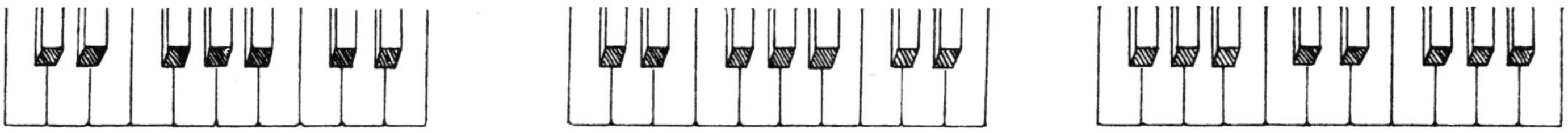

(*Write L.H. finger numbers on keyboard diagrams. See chart below.*)

KEYBOARD ASSIGNMENT

Right Hand

Left Hand

FINGERING AND INVERSION CHART

Left Hand | Right Hand

Root Position | First Inversion | Second Inversion | Root Position | First Inversion | Second Inversion

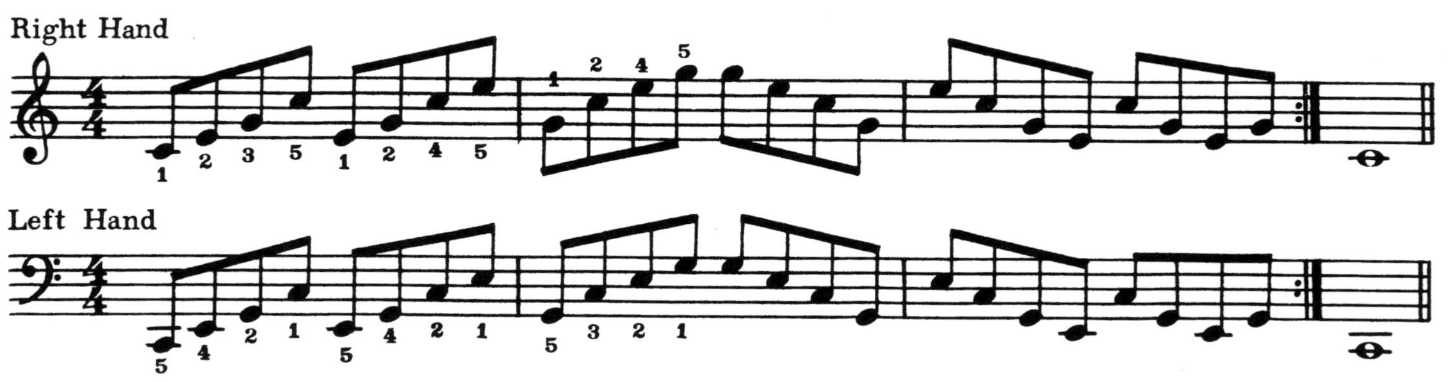

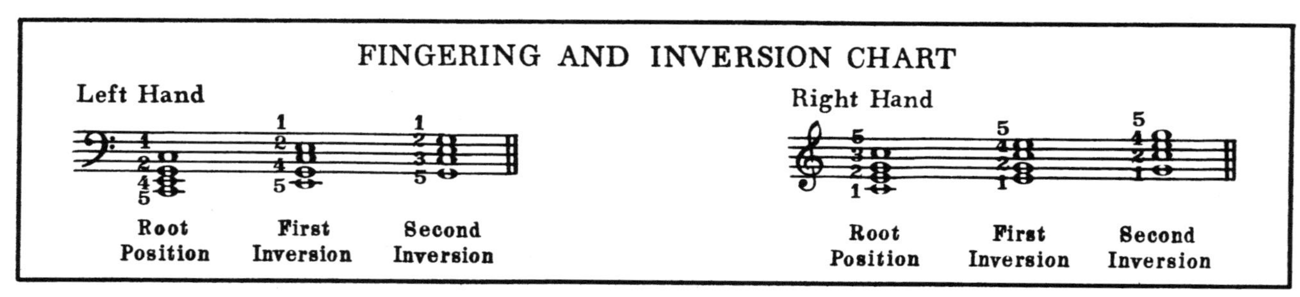

Lesson 2. G Major Arpeggio

Pupil's Name.. Completion Date..

Assignment Date.. Grade or Star..

DIRECTIONS: On the staffs below, write whole notes for the root position and inversions of the G major arpeggio. Consult chart at bottom of page.

Root Position   First Inversion   Second Inversion

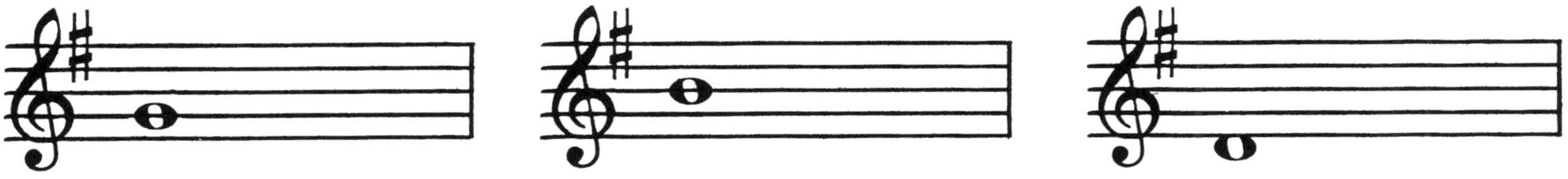

(Write letter names on dotted lines.)

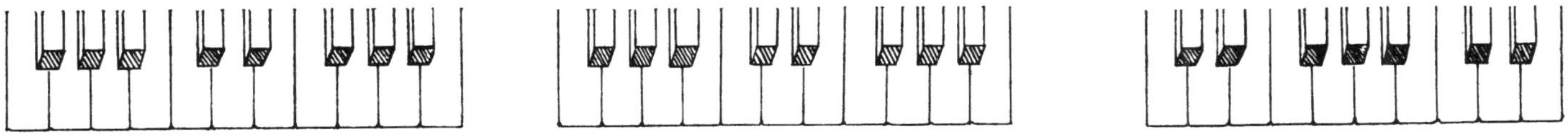

(Write R.H. finger numbers on keyboard diagrams. See chart below.)

Root Position   First Inversion   Second Inversion

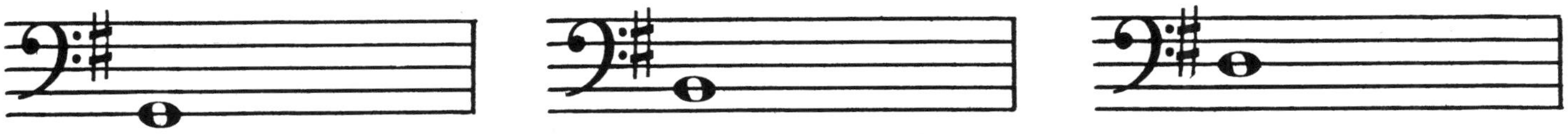

(Write letter names on dotted lines.)

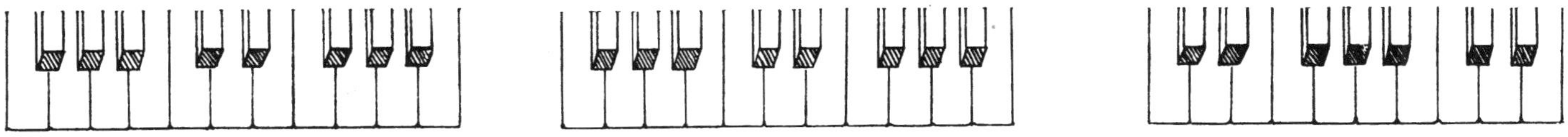

(Write L.H. finger numbers. See chart below.)

KEYBOARD ASSIGNMENT

Right Hand

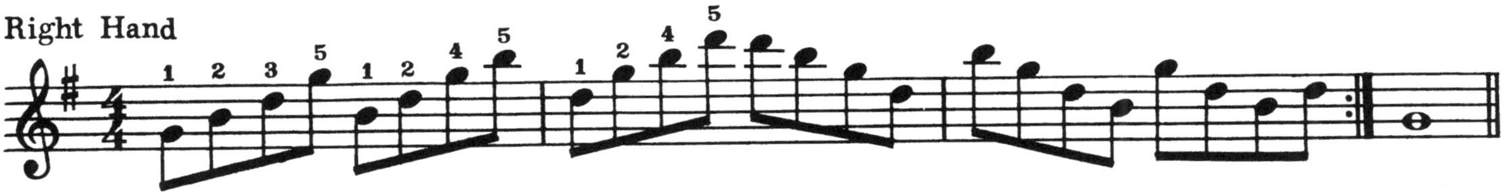

Left Hand

FINGERING AND INVERSION CHART

Left Hand

Root Position	First Inversion	Second Inversion

Right Hand

Root Position	First Inversion	Second Inversion

Lesson 3. D Major Arpeggio

Pupil's Name... Completion Date...

Assignment Date... Grade or Star...

DIRECTIONS: On the staffs below, write whole notes for the root position and inversions of the D major arpeggio. Consult chart at bottom of page.

Root Position   First Inversion   Second Inversion

(Write letter names.)

(Write R.H. finger numbers. See chart below.)

Root Position   First Inversion   Second Inversion

(Write letter names.)

(Write L.H. finger numbers. See chart below.)

KEYBOARD ASSIGNMENT

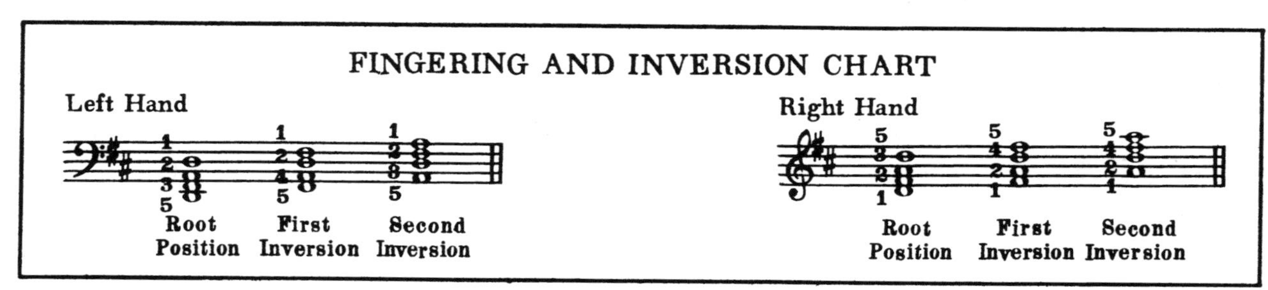

Lesson 4. A Major Arpeggio

Pupil's Name.. Completion Date..

Assignment Date.. Grade or Star..

DIRECTIONS: On the staffs below, write whole notes for the root position and inversions of the A major arpeggio. Consult chart at bottom of page.

Root Position	First Inversion	Second Inversion

(*Write letter names.*)

(*Write R.H. finger numbers. See Chart below.*)

Root Position	First Inversion	Second Inversion

(*Write letter names.*)

(*Write L.H. finger numbers. See Chart below.*)

KEYBOARD ASSIGNMENT

Right Hand

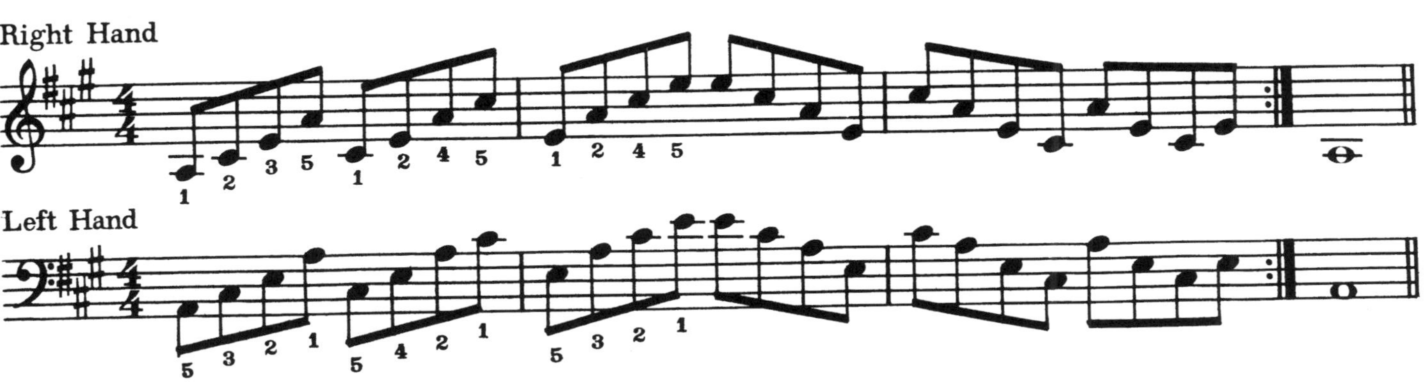

Left Hand

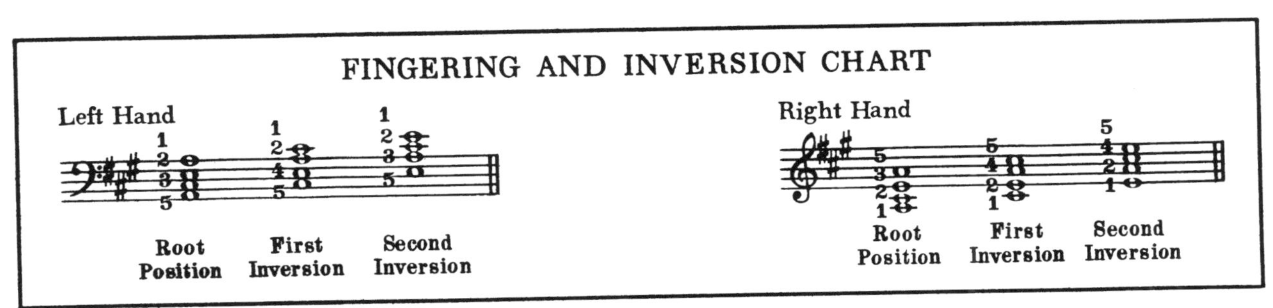

FINGERING AND INVERSION CHART

Left Hand

Root Position	First Inversion	Second Inversion

Right Hand

Root Position	First Inversion	Second Inversion

Lesson 5. E Major Arpeggio

Pupil's Name..   Completion Date..

Assignment Date..   Grade or Star..

DIRECTIONS: On the staffs below, write whole notes for the root position and inversions of the E major arpeggio. Consult chart at bottom of page.

Root Position   First Inversion   Second Inversion

(*Write letter names.*)

(*Write R.H. finger numbers. See chart below.*)

Root Position   First Inversion   Second Inversion

(*Write letter names.*)

(*Write L.H. finger numbers. See chart below.*)

KEYBOARD ASSIGNMENT

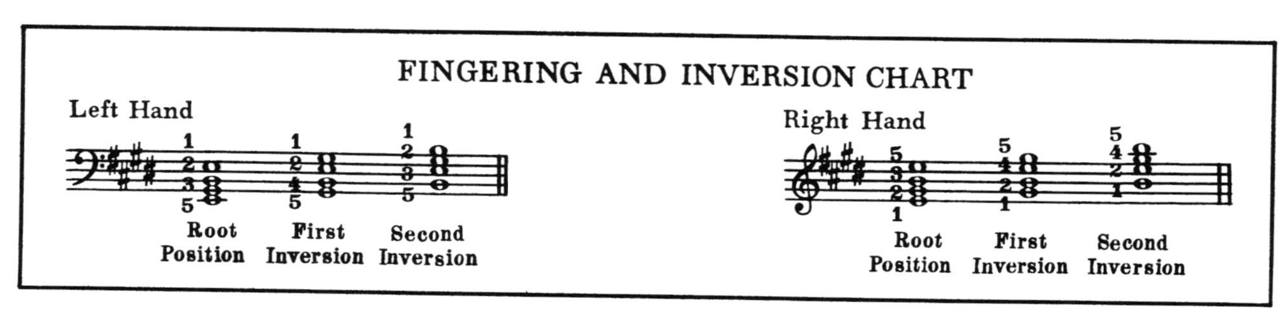

FINGERING AND INVERSION CHART

Left Hand   Right Hand

Lesson 6. B Major Arpeggio

Pupil's Name..

Assignment Date..

Completion Date...

Grade or Star..

DIRECTIONS: On the staffs below, write whole notes for the root position and inversions of the B major arpeggio. Consult chart at bottom of page.

Root Position   First Inversion   Second Inversion

(Write letter names.)

(Write R.H. finger numbers. See chart below.)

Root Position   First Inversion   Second Inversion

(Write letter names.)

(Write L.H. finger numbers. See chart below.)

KEYBOARD ASSIGNMENT

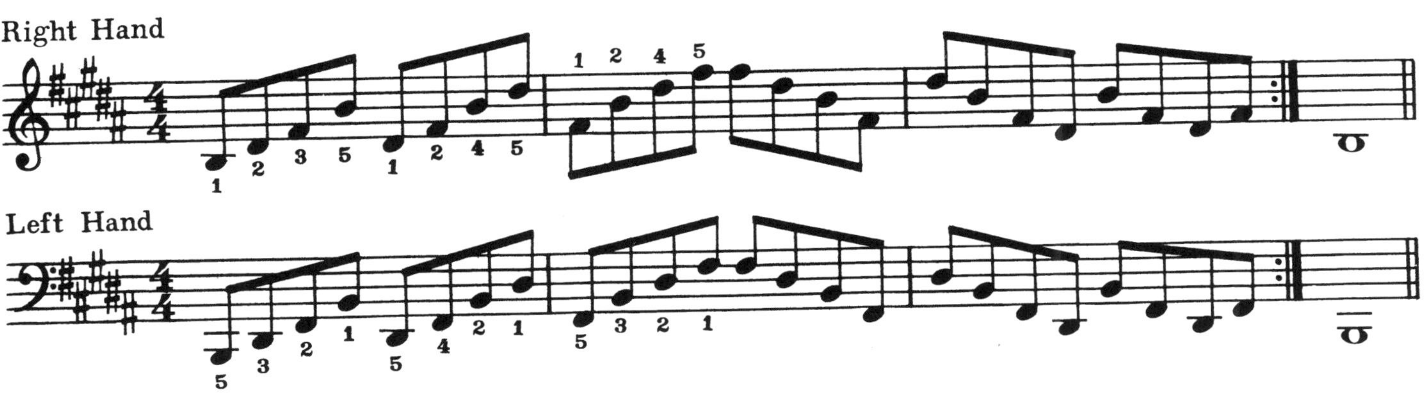

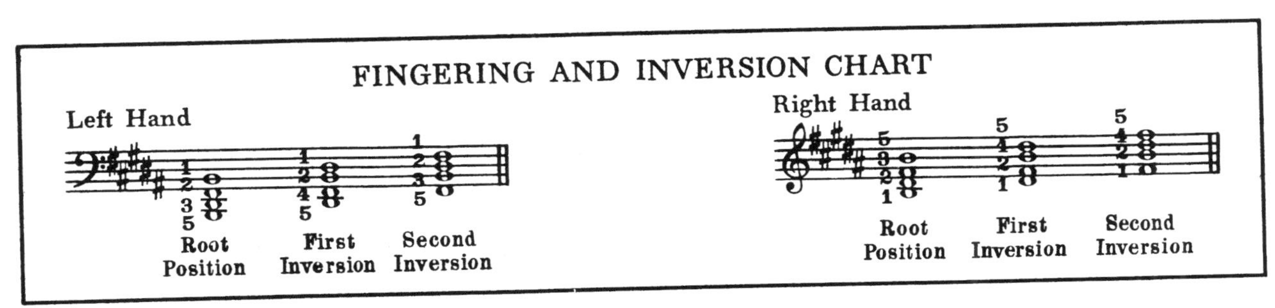

FINGERING AND INVERSION CHART

Lesson 7. Arpeggio Quiz No. 1

DIRECTIONS: Match each arpeggio at the left with the corresponding chord position at the right by inserting the correct alphabetical letter on the proper dotted line. For example, the answer to No. 1 is the "First inversion of G major," therefore, the letter *j* has been placed on the dotted line.

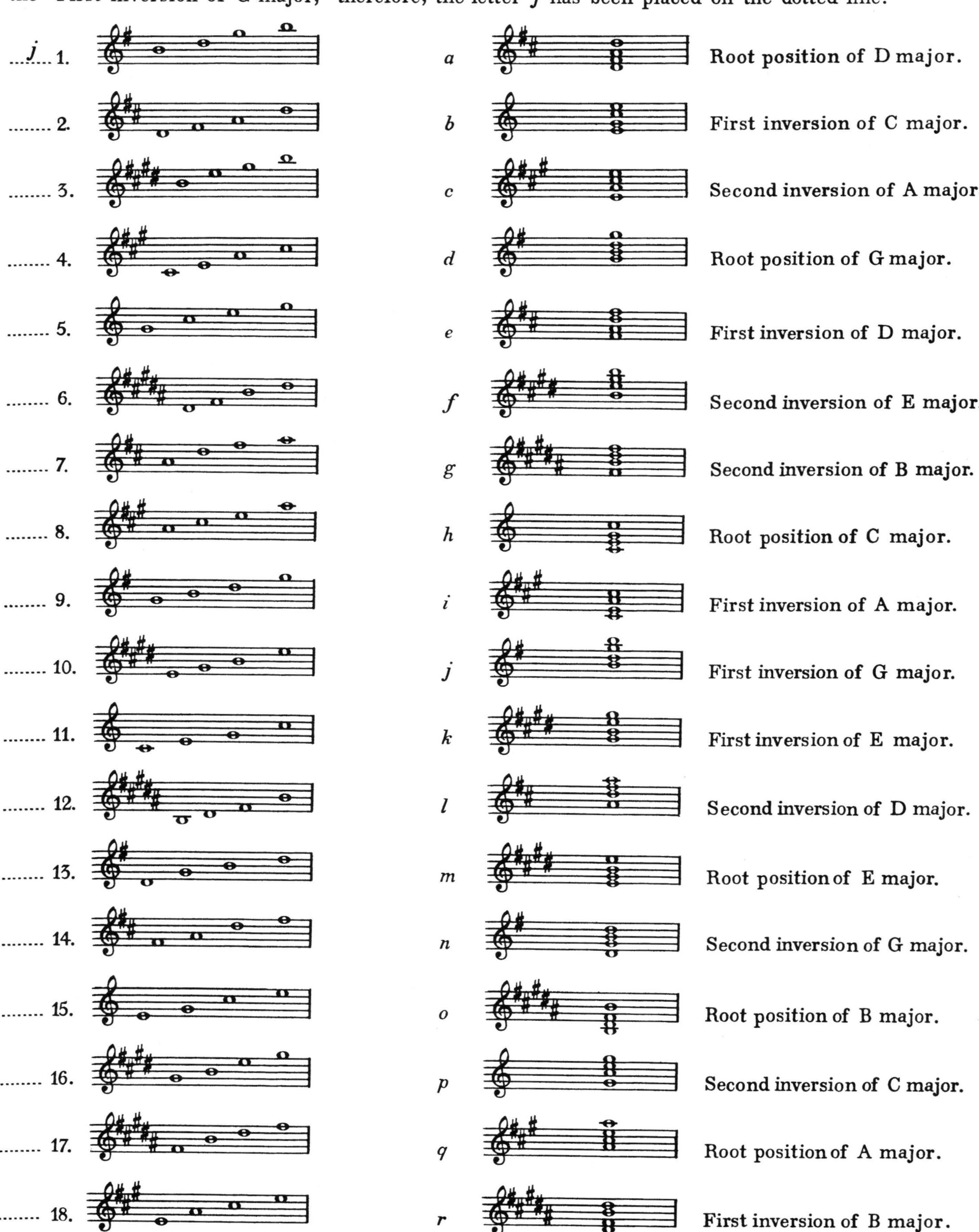

Lesson 8. F Major Arpeggio

Pupil's Name.. Completion Date..

Assignment Date.. Grade or Star..

DIRECTIONS: On the staffs below, write whole notes for the root position and inversions of the F major arpeggio. Consult chart at bottom of page.

Root Position   First Inversion   Second Inversion

(Write letter names.)

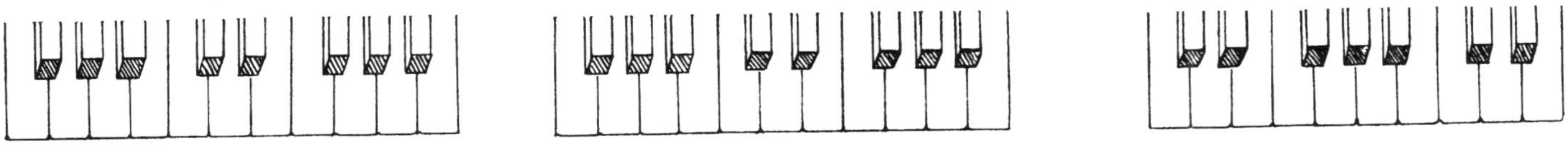

(Write R.H. finger numbers. See chart below.)

Root Position   First Inversion   Second Inversion

(Write letter names.)

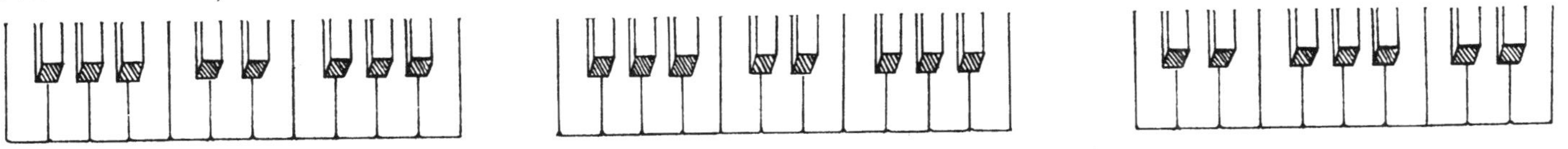

(Write L.H. finger numbers. See chart below.)

KEYBOARD ASSIGNMENT

Right Hand

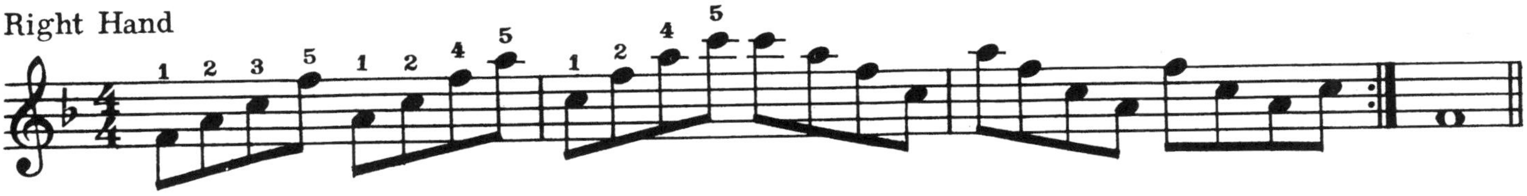

Left Hand

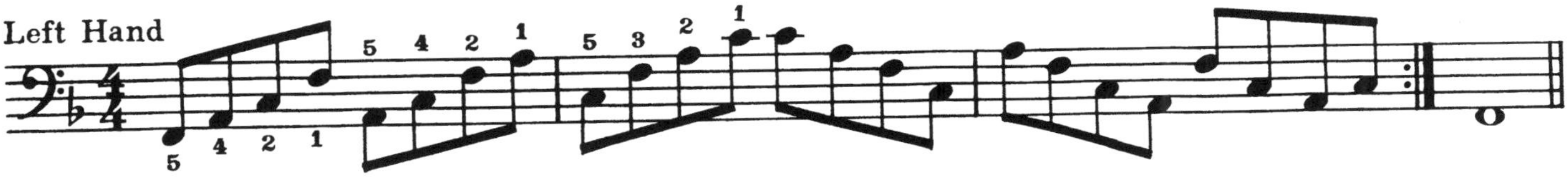

FINGERING AND INVERSION CHART

Left Hand

Right Hand

Root Position   First Inversion   Second Inversion

Root Position   First Inversion   Second Inversion

Lesson 9. B Flat Major Arpeggio

Pupil's Name... *Completion Date*...

Assignment Date... *Grade or Star*...

DIRECTIONS: On the staffs below, write whole notes for the root position and inversions of the B♭ major arpeggio. Consult chart at bottom of page.

Root Position First Inversion Second Inversion

(Write letter names.)

(Write R.H. finger numbers. See chart below.)

Root Position First Inversion Second Inversion

(Write letter names.)

(Write L.H. finger numbers. See chart below.)

KEYBOARD ASSIGNMENT

Right Hand

Left Hand

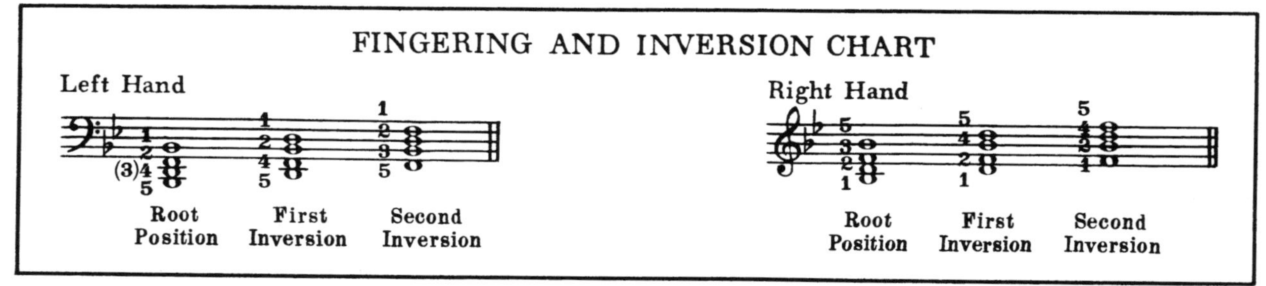

Lesson 10. E Flat Major Arpeggio

Pupil's Name.. **Completion Date**..

Assignment Date.. **Grade or Star**..

DIRECTIONS: On the staffs below, write whole notes for the root position and inversions of the E♭ major arpeggio. Consult chart at bottom of page.

Root Position   First Inversion   Second Inversion

(Write letter names.)

(Write R.H. finger numbers. See chart below.)

Root Position   First Inversion   Second Inversion

(Write letter names.)

(Write L.H. finger numbers. See chart below.)

KEYBOARD ASSIGNMENT

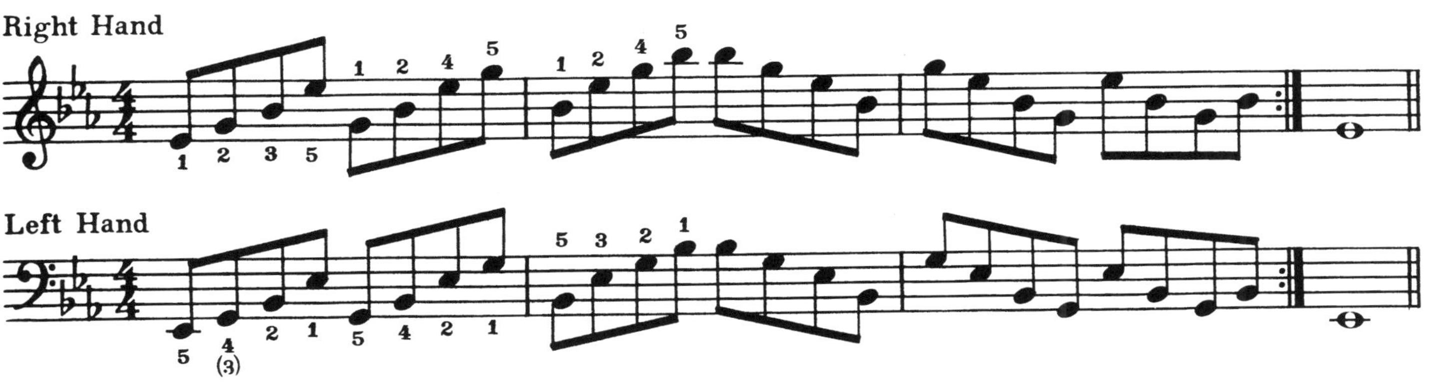

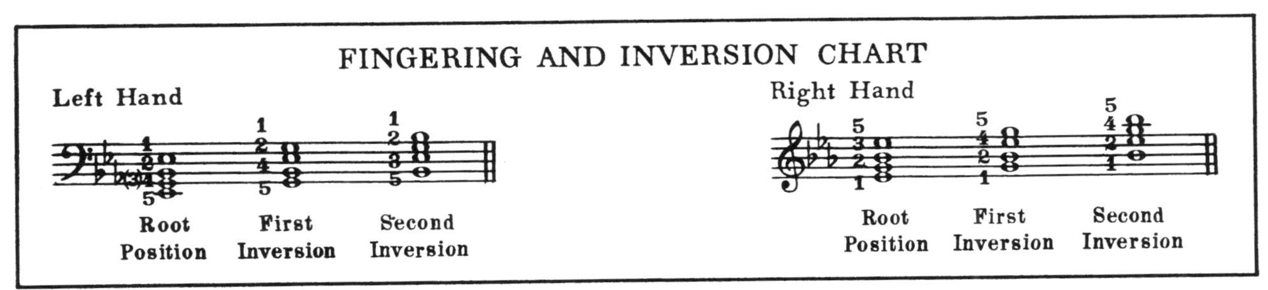

Lesson 11. A Flat Major Arpeggio

Pupil's Name.. Completion Date..

Assignment Date.. Grade or Star..

DIRECTIONS: On the staffs below, write whole notes for the root position and inversions of the A♭ major arpeggio. Consult chart at bottom of page.

Root Position — First Inversion — Second Inversion

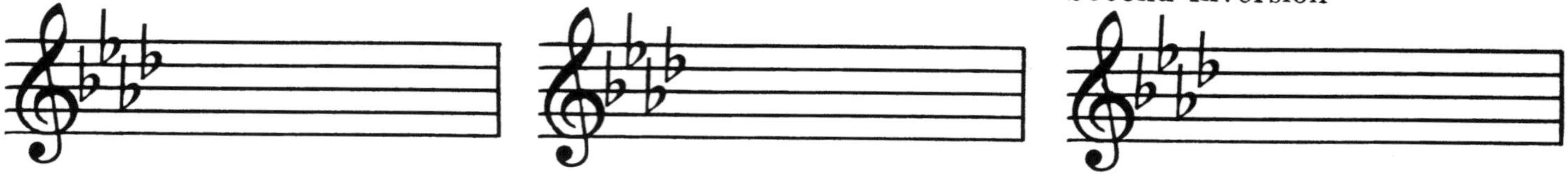

....

(Write letter names.)

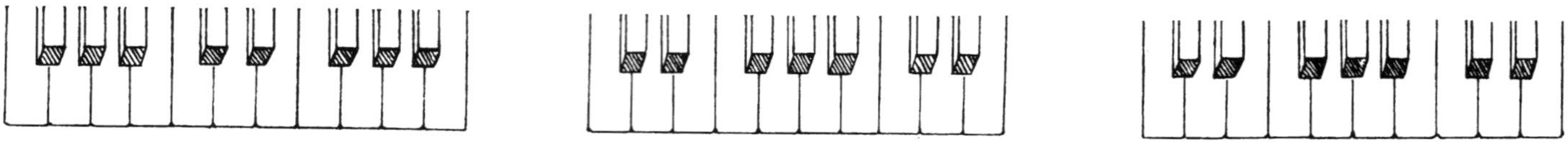

(Write R.H. finger numbers. See chart below.)

Root Position — First Inversion — Second Inversion

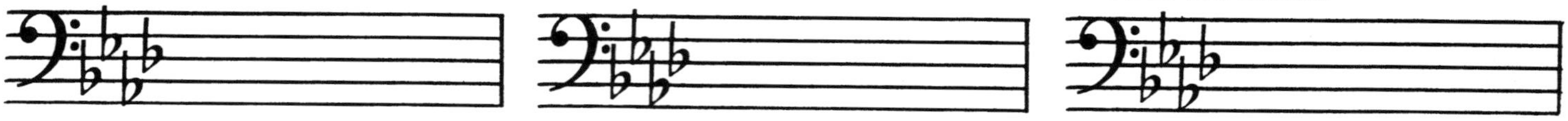

....

(Write letter names.)

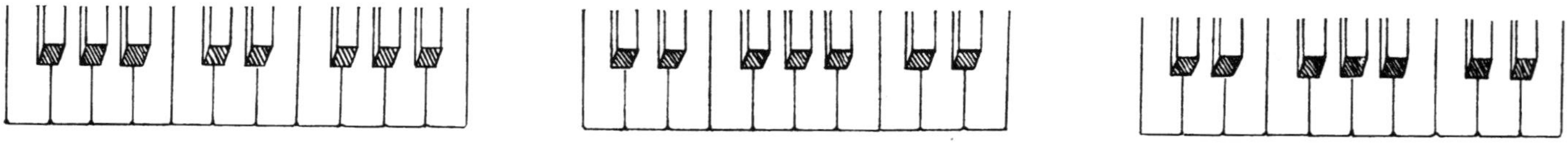

(Write L.H. finger numbers. See chart below.)

KEYBOARD ASSIGNMENT

Right Hand

Left Hand

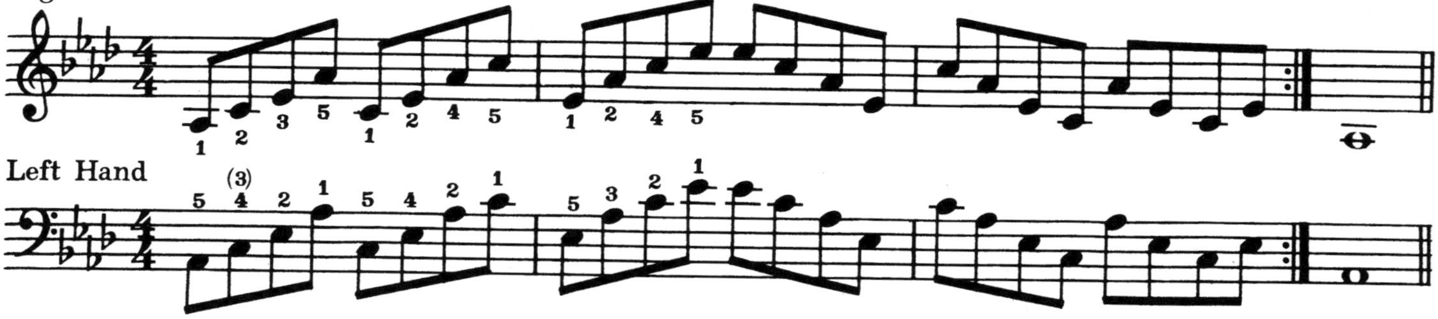

FINGERING AND INVERSION CHART

Left Hand

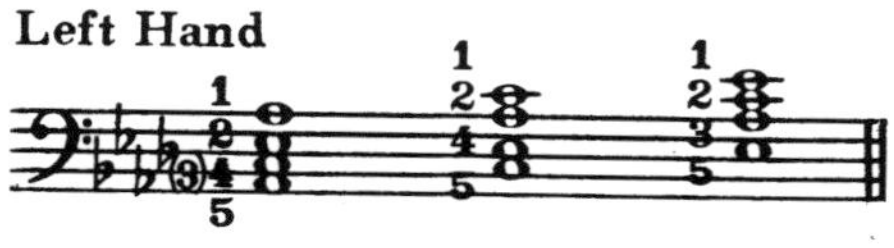

Root Position — First Inversion — Second Inversion

Right Hand

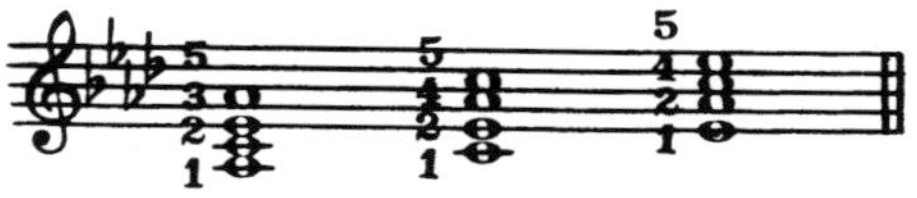

Root Position — First Inversion — Second Inversion

Lesson 12. D Flat Major Arpeggio

Pupil's Name..   Completion Date..

Assignment Date..   Grade or Star..

DIRECTIONS: On the staffs below, write whole notes for the root position and inversions of the D♭ major arpeggio. Consult chart at bottom of page.

Root Position   First Inversion   Second Inversion

(Write letter names.)

(Write R.H. finger numbers. See chart below.)

Root Position   First Inversion   Second Inversion

(Write letter names.)

(Write L.H. finger numbers. See chart below.)

KEYBOARD ASSIGNMENT

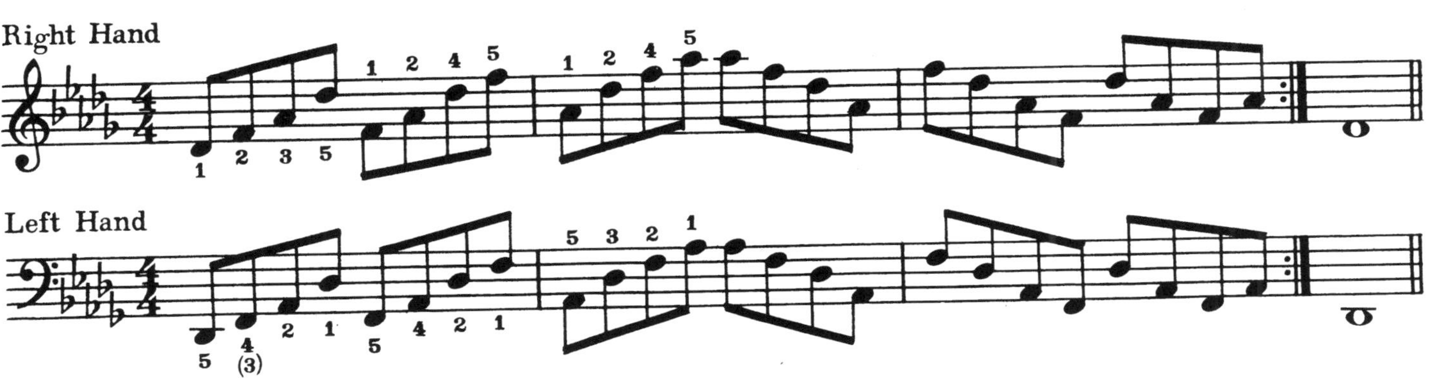

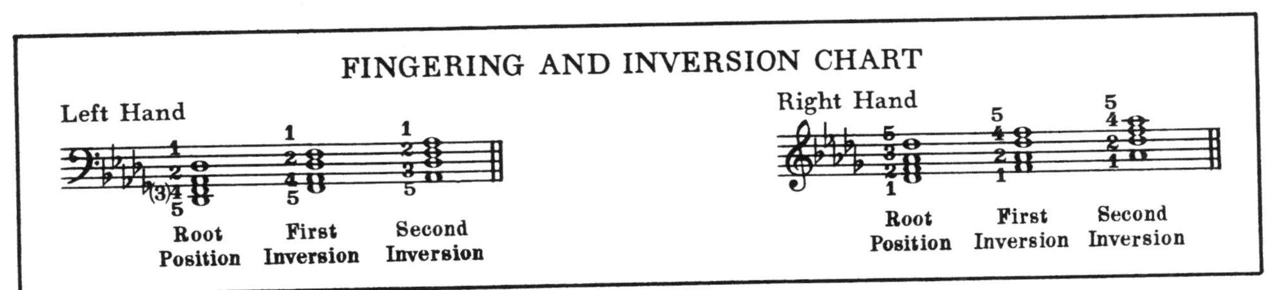

Lesson 13. G Flat Major Arpeggio

Pupil's Name.. Completion Date..

Assignment Date.. Grade or Star..

DIRECTIONS: On the staffs below, write whole notes for the root position and inversions of the G♭ major arpeggio. Consult chart at bottom of page.

Root Position First Inversion Second Inversion

(Write letter names.)

(Write L.H. finger numbers. See chart below.)

Root Position First Inversion Second Inversion

(Write letter names.)

(Write R.H. finger numbers. See chart below.)

KEYBOARD ASSIGNMENT

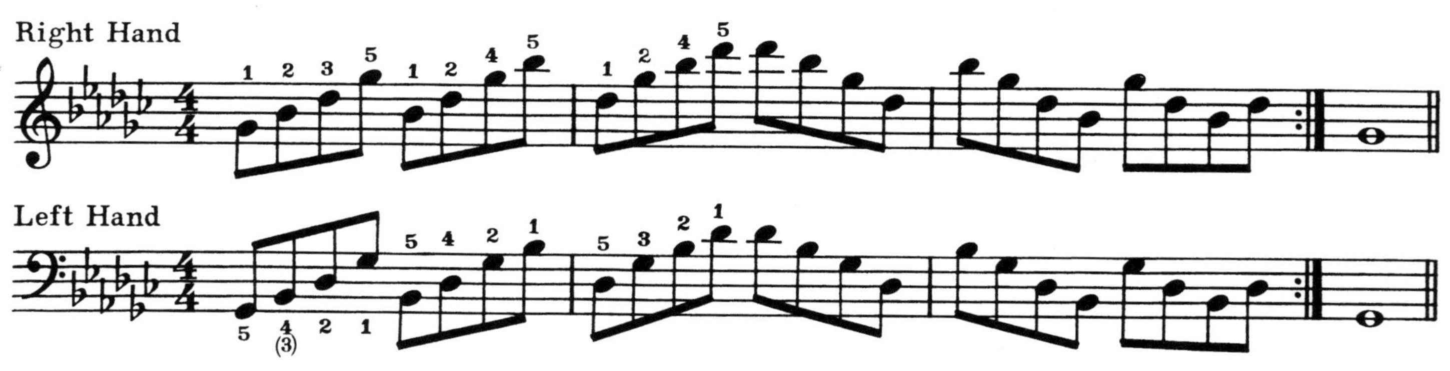

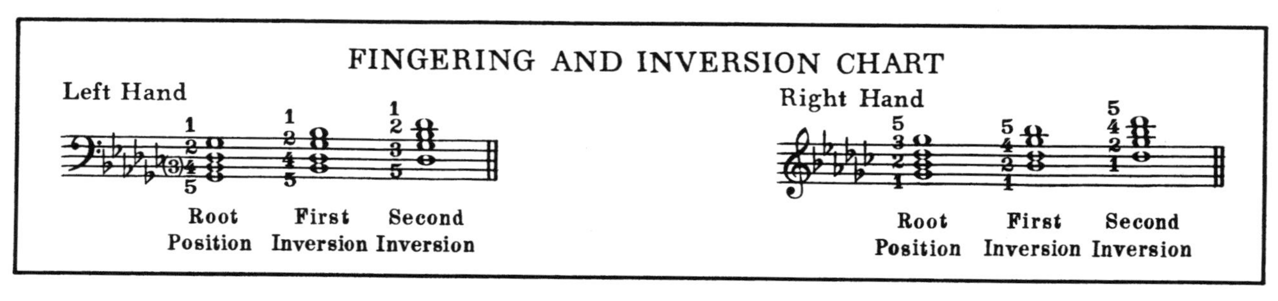

Lesson 14. Arpeggio Quiz No. 2

Pupil's Name.. **Completion Date**..

Assignment Date.. **Grade or Star**..

DIRECTIONS: Match each arpeggio at the left with the corresponding chord position at the right by inserting the correct alphabetical letter on the proper dotted line. For example, the answer to No.1 is the "First inversion of E♭ major," therefore, the letter *d* has been placed on the dotted line.

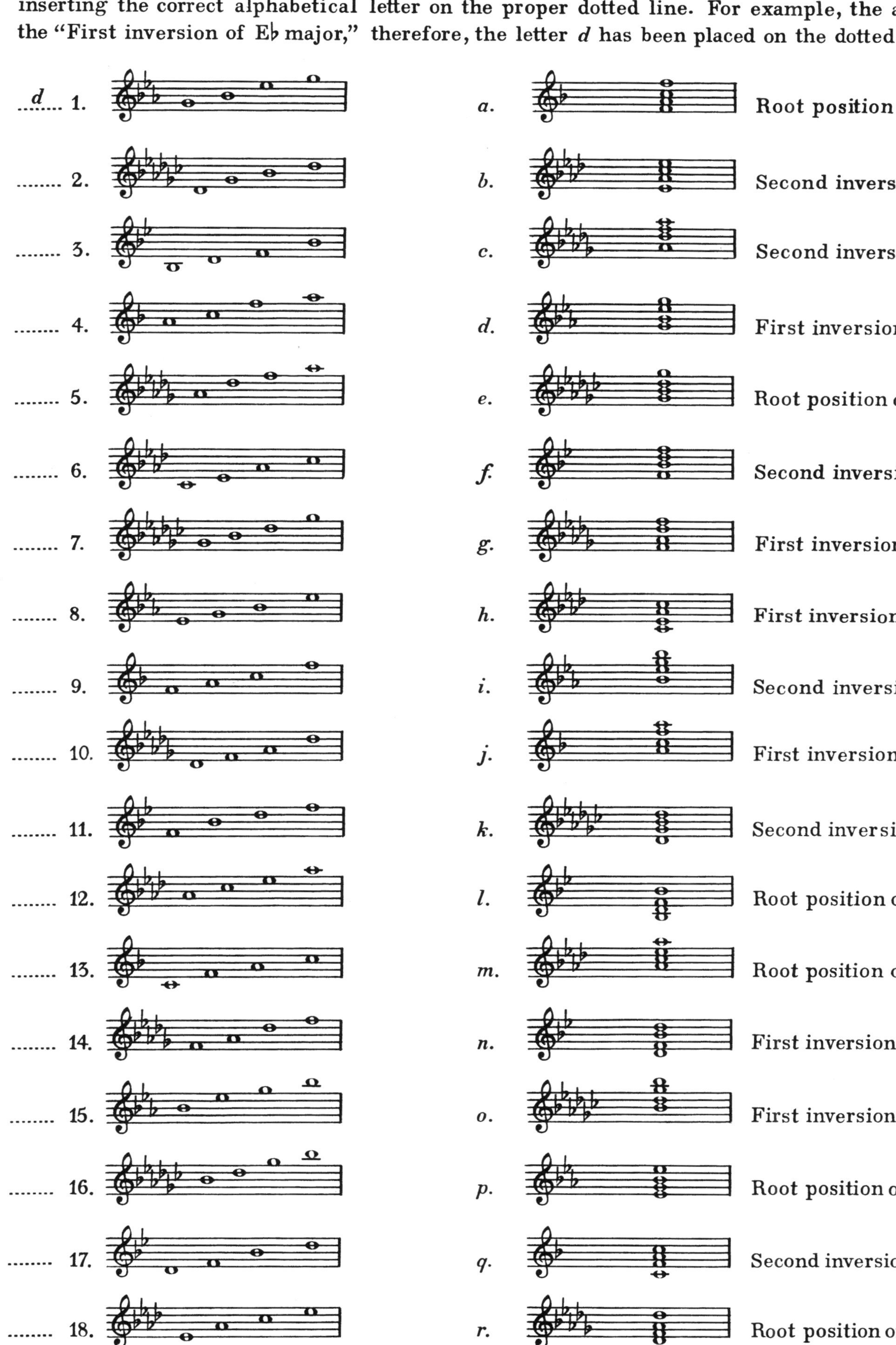

Lesson 15. A Minor Arpeggio

Pupil's Name..

Assignment Date..

Completion Date..

Grade or Star..

DIRECTIONS: On the staffs below, write whole notes for the root position and inversions of the A minor arpeggio. See chart at bottom of page.

Root Position

First Inversion

Second Inversion

(Write letter names.)

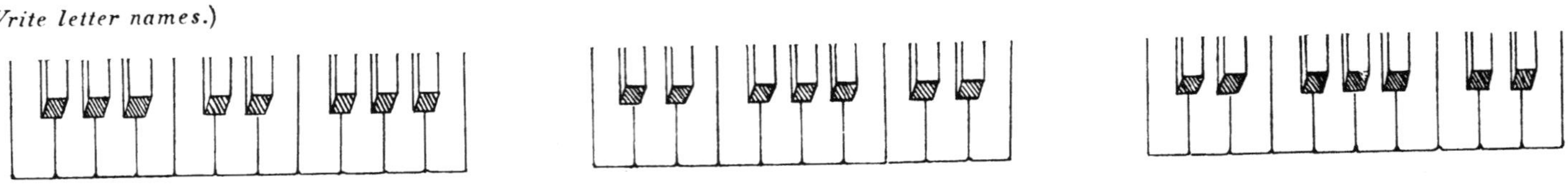

(Write R.H. finger numbers. See chart below.)

Root Position

First Inversion

Second Inversion

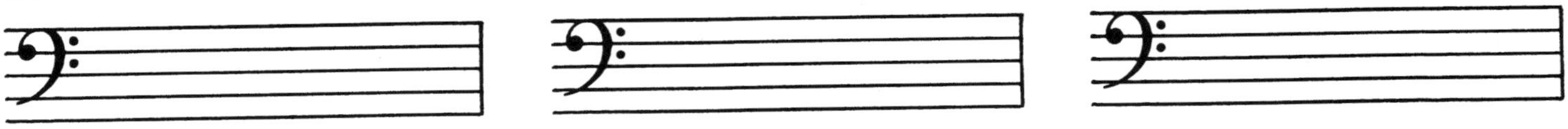

(Write letter names.)

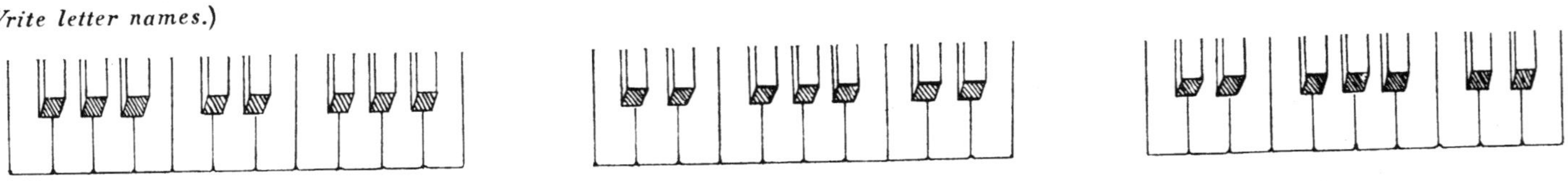

(Write L.H. finger numbers. See chart below.)

KEYBOARD ASSIGNMENT

Right Hand

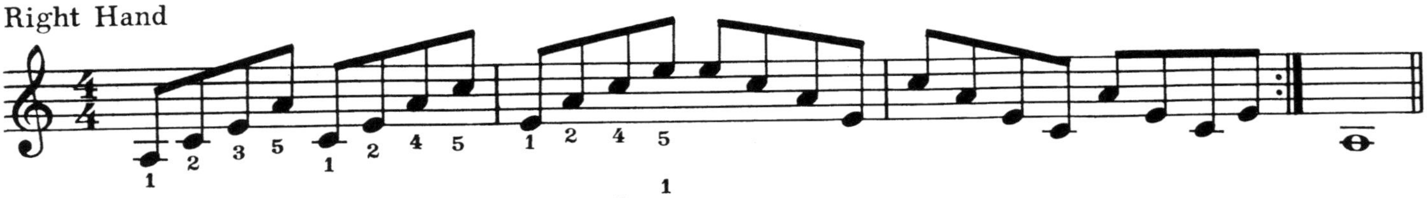

Left Hand

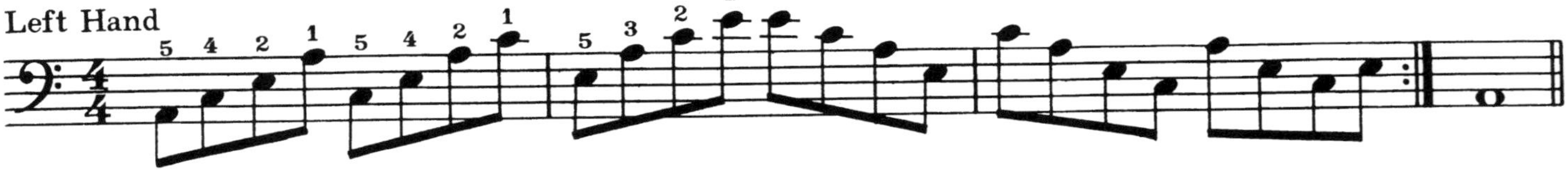

FINGERING AND INVERSION CHART

Left Hand

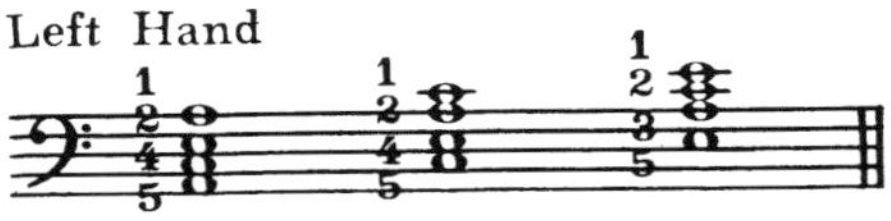

Right Hand

Root Position   First Inversion   Second Inversion

Root Position   First Inversion   Second Inversion

Lesson 16. E Minor Arpeggio

Pupil's Name..

Completion Date..

Assignment Date..

Grade or Star..

DIRECTIONS: On the staffs below, write whole notes for the root position and inversions of the E minor arpeggio. See chart at bottom of page.

Root Position

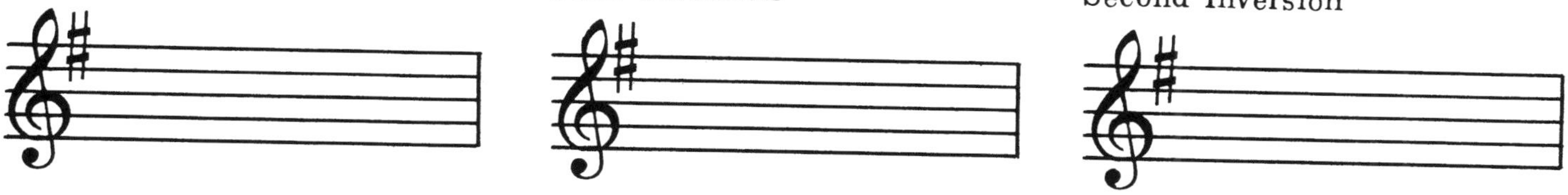

(Write letter names.)

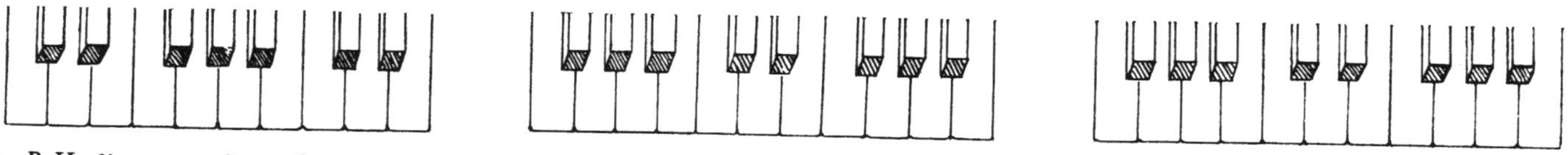

(Write R.H. finger numbers. See chart below.)

First Inversion

Second Inversion

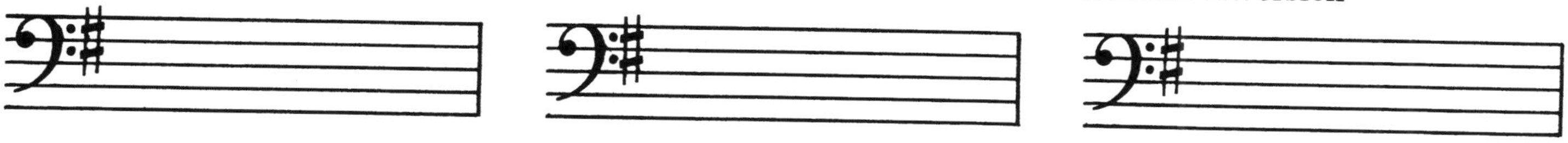

Root Position

(Write letter names.)

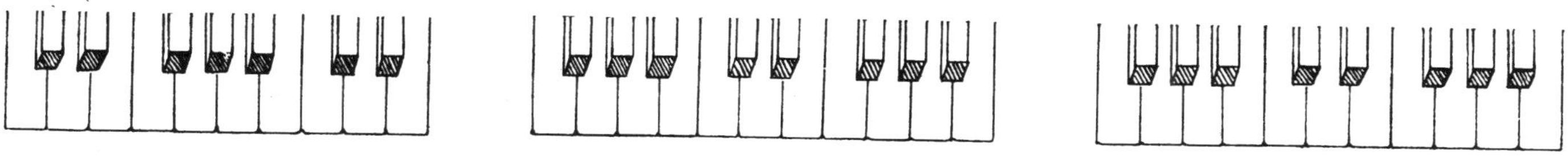

(Write L.H. finger numbers. See chart below.)

First Inversion

Second Inversion

KEYBOARD ASSIGNMENT

Right Hand

Left Hand

FINGERING AND INVERSION CHART

Left Hand

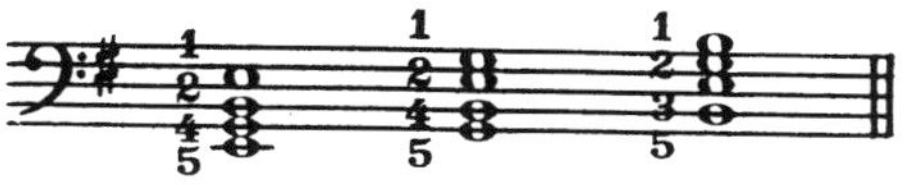

Root Position	First Inversion	Second Inversion

Right Hand

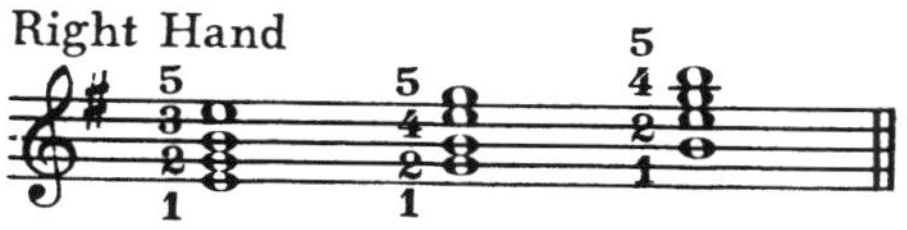

Root Position	First Inversion	Second Inversion

Lesson 17. B Minor Arpeggio

Pupil's Name...

Assignment Date...

Completion Date...

Grade or Star..

DIRECTIONS: On the staffs below, write whole notes for the root position and inversions of the B minor arpeggio. See chart at bottom of page.

Root Position

First Inversion

Second Inversion

(Write letter names.)

(Write R.H. finger numbers. See chart below.)

Root Position

First Inversion

Second Inversion

(Write letter names.)

(Write L.H. finger numbers. See chart below.)

KEYBOARD ASSIGNMENT

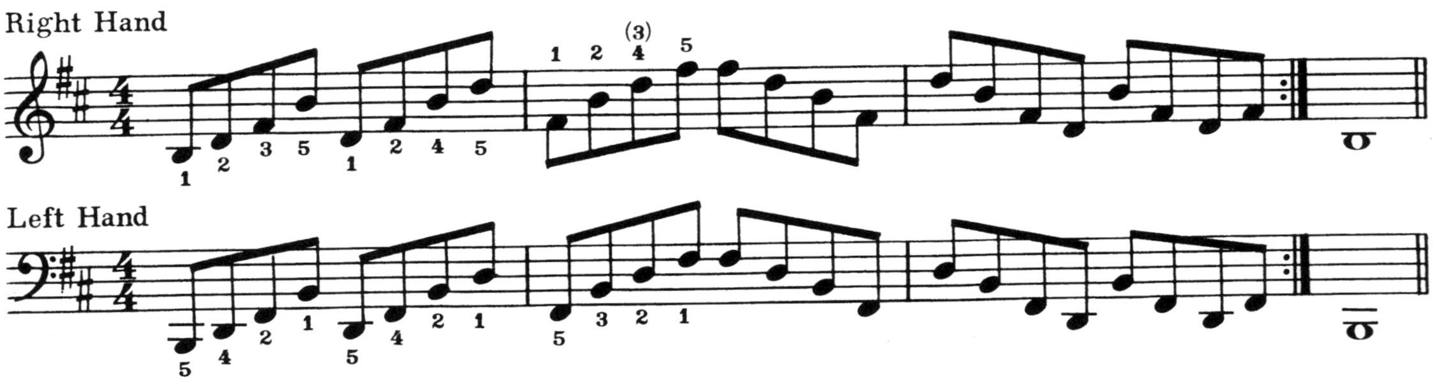

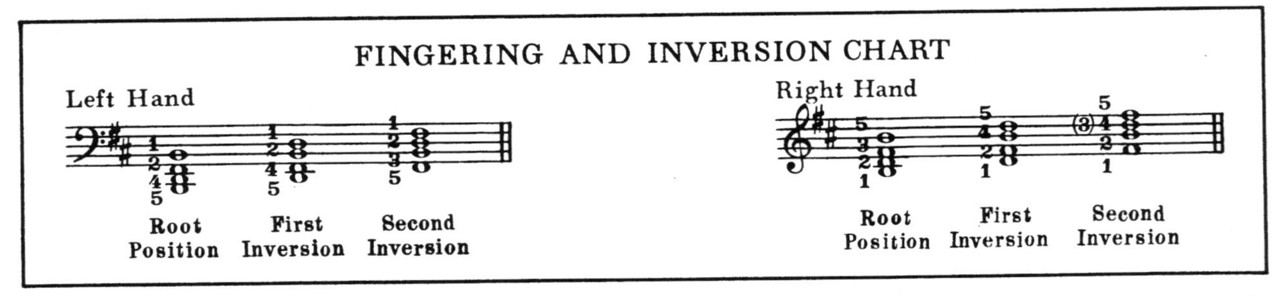

FINGERING AND INVERSION CHART

Lesson 18. F Sharp Minor Arpeggio

Pupil's Name..   Completion Date..

Assignment Date..   Grade or Star..

DIRECTIONS: On the staffs below, write whole notes for the root position and inversions of the F♯ minor arpeggio. See chart at bottom of page.

Root Position   First Inversion   Second Inversion

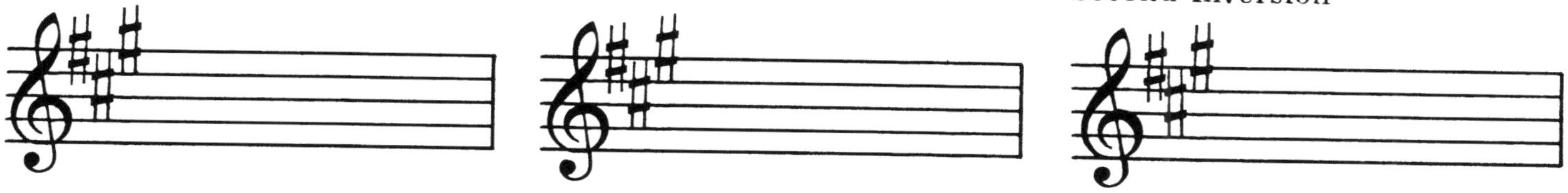

(*Write letter names.*)

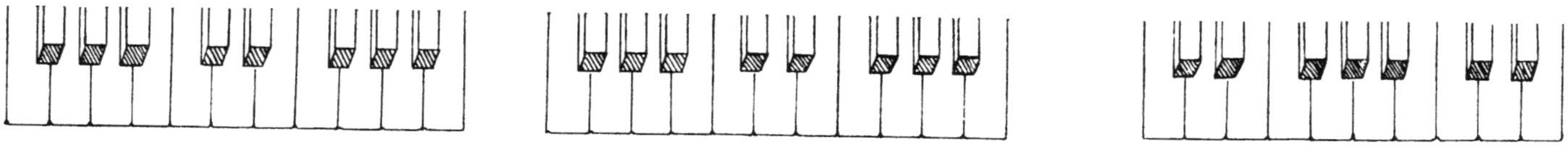

(*Write R.H. finger numbers. See chart below.*)

Root Position   First Inversion   Second Inversion

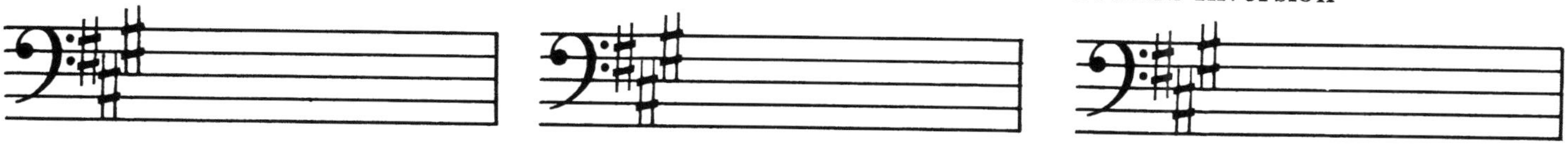

(*Write letter names.*)

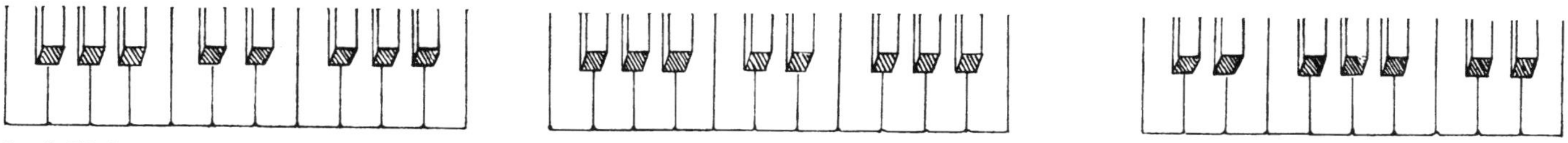

(*Write L.H. finger numbers. See chart below*)

KEYBOARD ASSIGNMENT

Right Hand

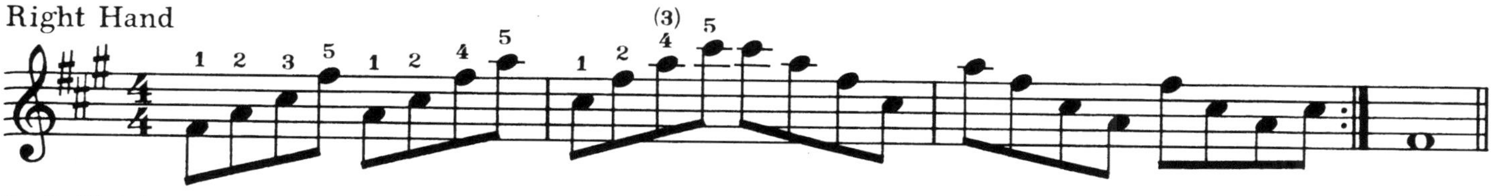

Left Hand

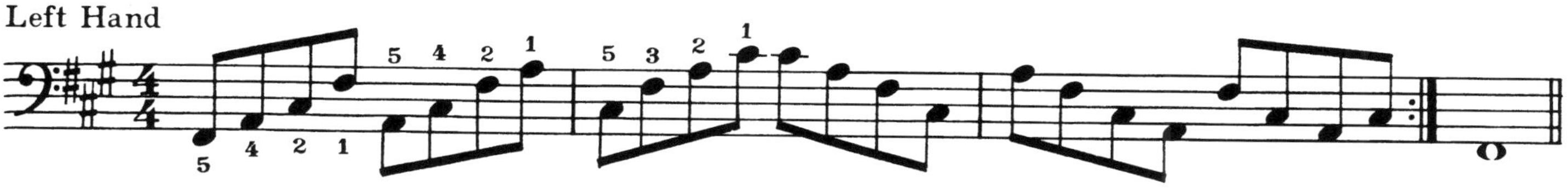

FINGERING AND INVERSION CHART

Left Hand

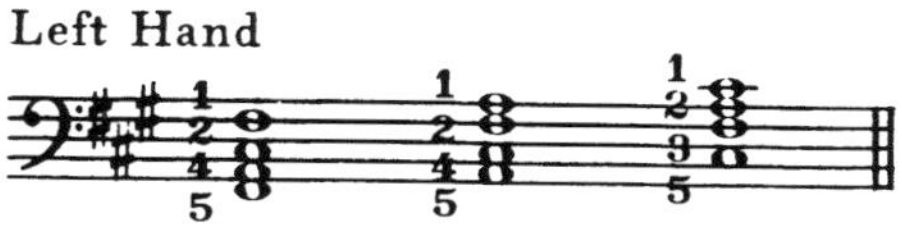

Root Position	First Inversion	Second Inversion

Right Hand

Root Position	First Inversion	Second Inversion

Lesson 19. C Sharp Minor Arpeggio

Pupil's Name..

Assignment Date...

Completion Date..

Grade or Star...

DIRECTIONS: On the staffs below, write whole notes for the root position and inversions of the C# minor arpeggio. See chart at bottom of page.

Root Position

First Inversion

Second Inversion

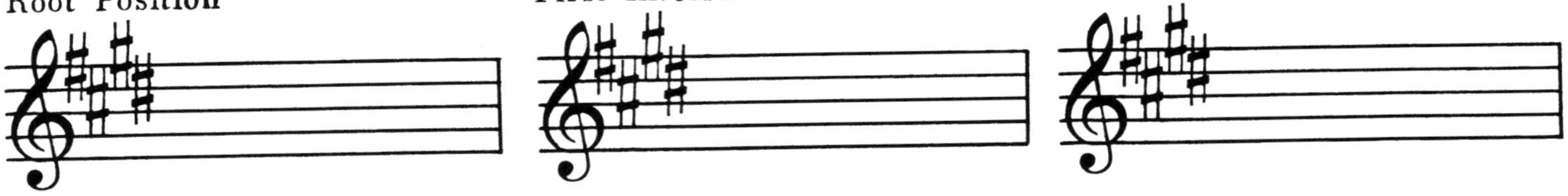

(Write letter names.)

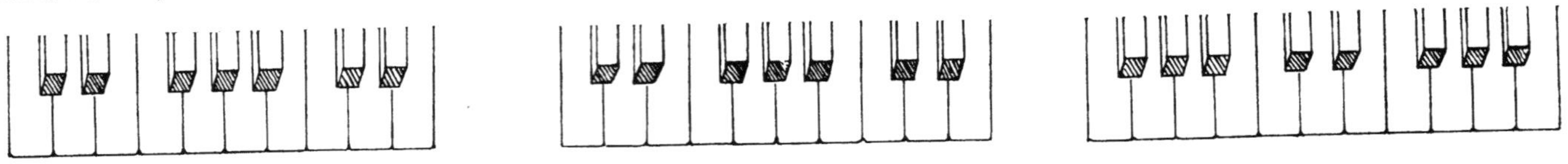

(Write R.H. finger numbers. See chart below.)

Root Position

First Inversion

Second Inversion

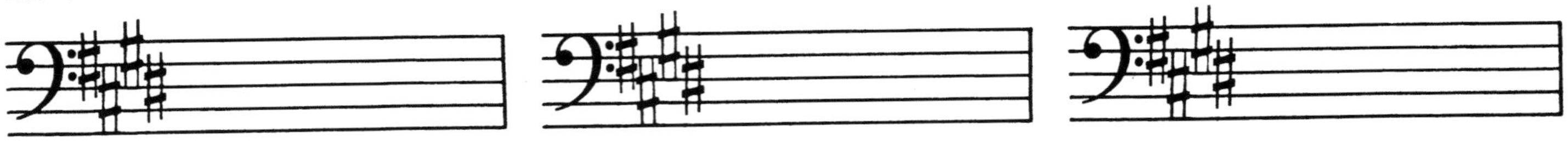

(Write letter names.)

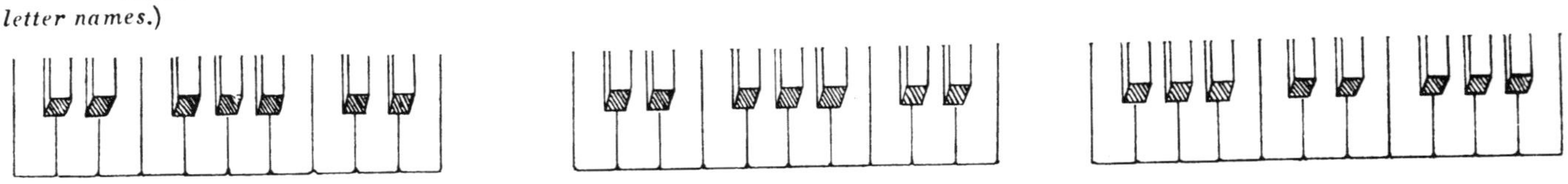

(Write L.H. finger numbers. See chart below.)

KEYBOARD ASSIGNMENT

Right Hand

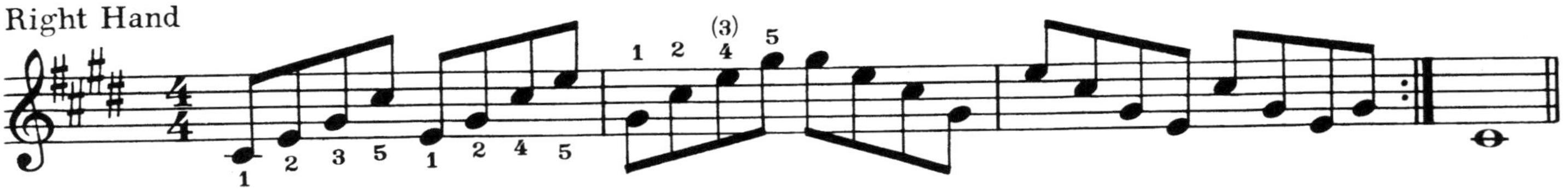

Left Hand

FINGERING AND INVERSION CHART

Left Hand

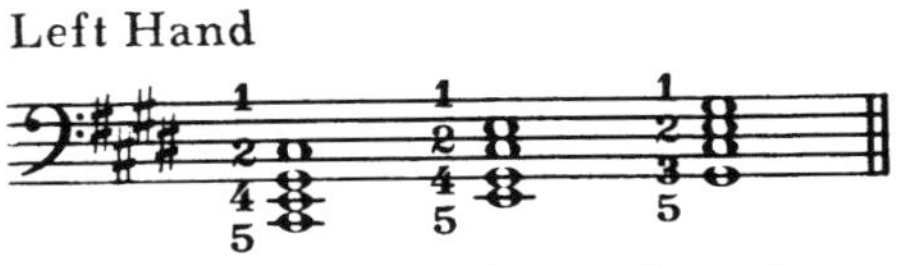

Right Hand

Root   First   Second
Position   Inversion   Inversion

Root   First   Second
Position   Inversion   Inversion

Lesson 20. G Sharp Minor Arpeggio

Pupil's Name... Completion Date...

Assignment Date... Grade or Star...

DIRECTIONS: On the staffs below, write whole notes for the root position and inversions of the G♯ minor arpeggio. See chart at bottom of page.

Root Position   **First Inversion**   **Second Inversion**

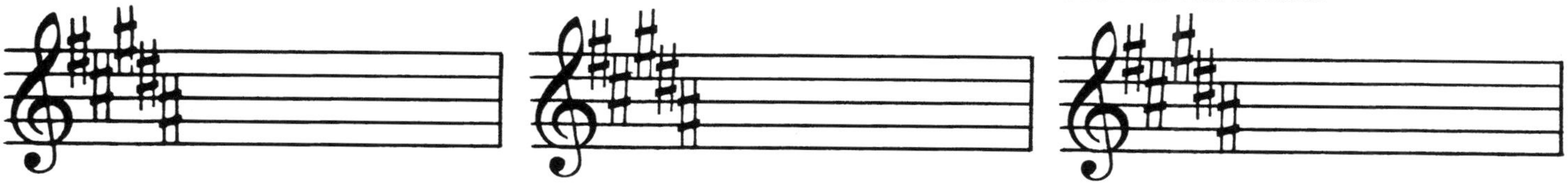

(Write letter names.)

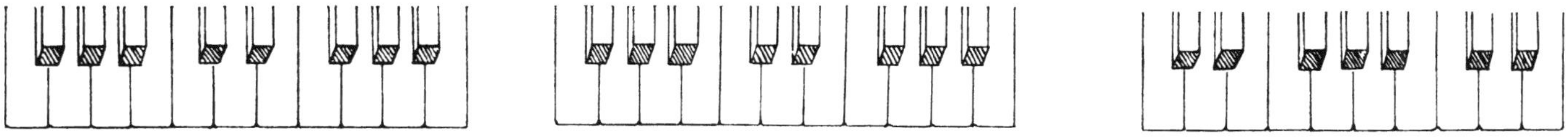

(Write R.H. finger numbers. See chart below.)

Root Position   **First Inversion**   **Second Inversion**

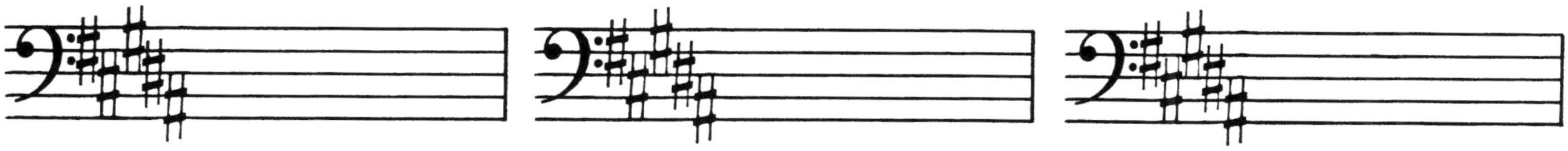

(Write letter names.)

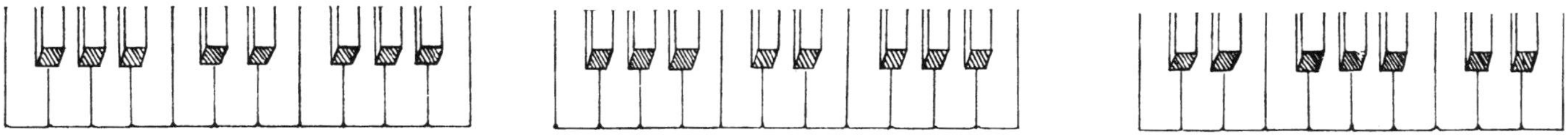

(Write L.H. finger numbers. See chart below.)

KEYBOARD ASSIGNMENT

Right Hand

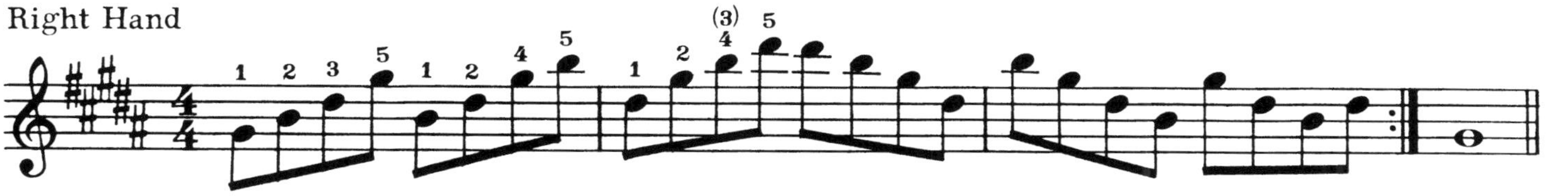

Left Hand

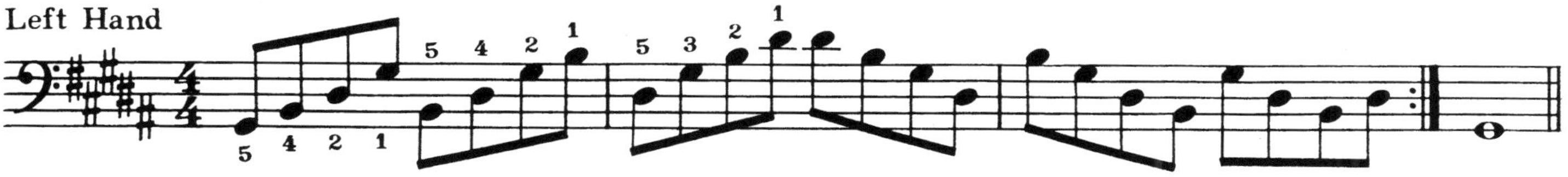

FINGERING AND INVERSION CHART

Left Hand

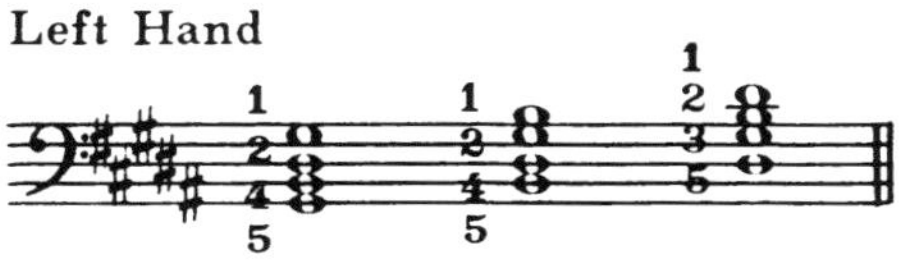

Root Position	First Inversion	Second Inversion

Right Hand

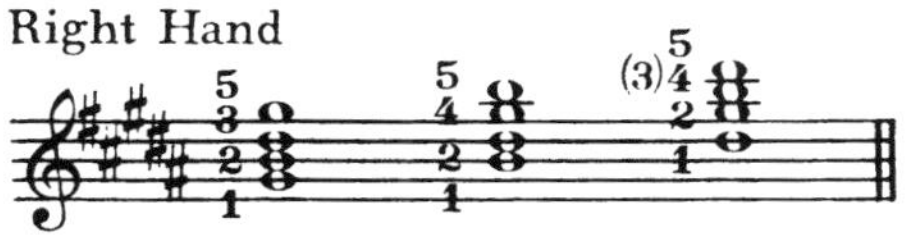

Root Position	First Inversion	Second Inversion

Lesson 21. Arpeggio Quiz No. 3

Pupil's Name...

Assignment Date...

Completion Date..

Grade or Star..

DIRECTIONS: Match each arpeggio at the left with the corresponding chord position at the right by inserting the correct alphabetical letter on the proper dotted line. For example, the answer to No.1 is the "First inversion of B minor," therefore, the letter *e* has been placed on the dotted line.

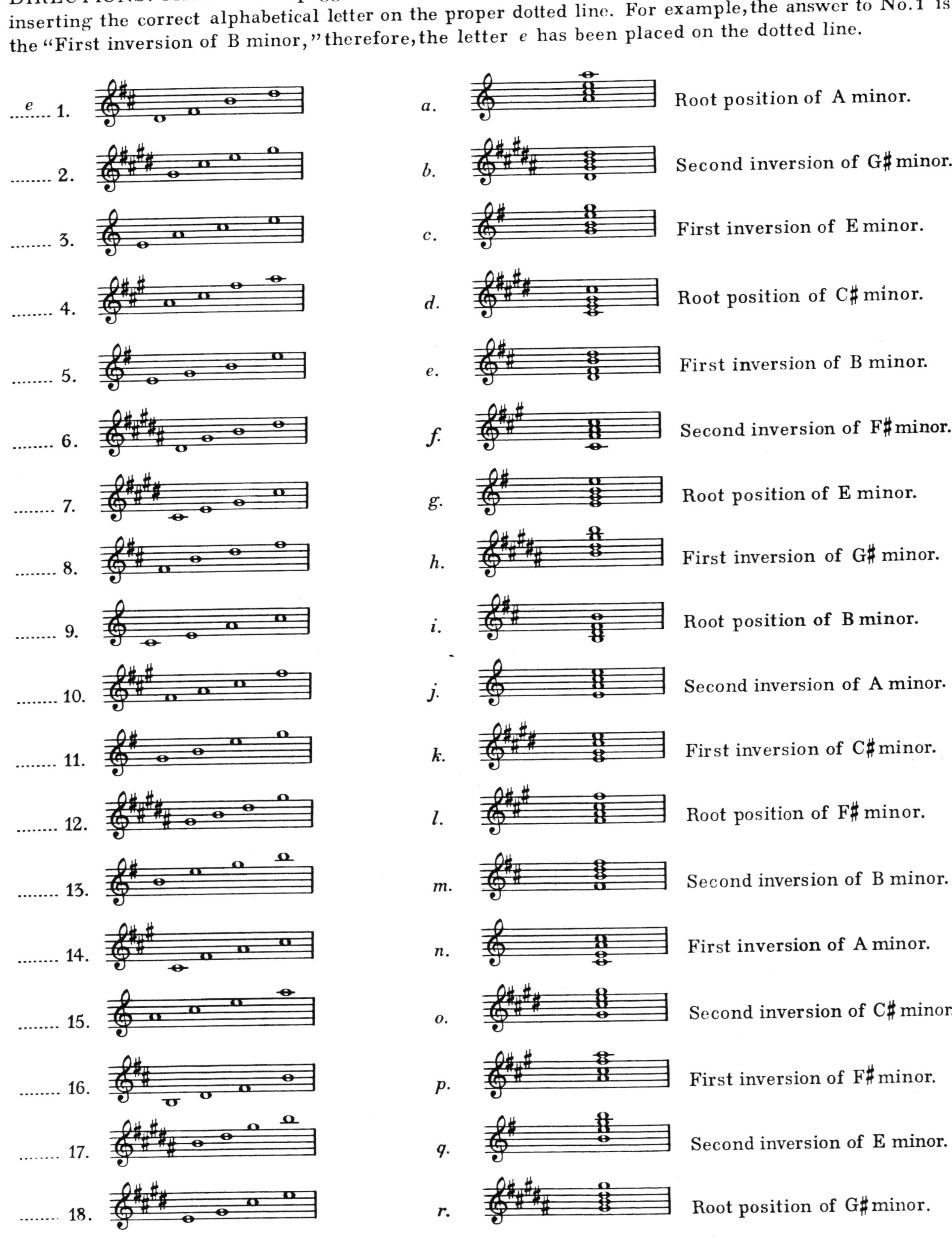

Lesson 22. D Minor Arpeggio

Pupil's Name .... *Completion Date* ....

Assignment Date .... *Grade or Star* ....

DIRECTIONS: On the staffs below, write whole notes for the root position and inversions of the D minor arpeggio. See chart at bottom of page.

Root Position | First Inversion | Second Inversion

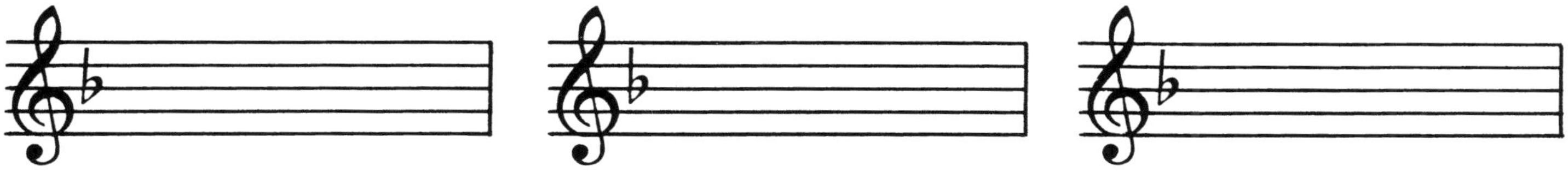

(Write letter names.)

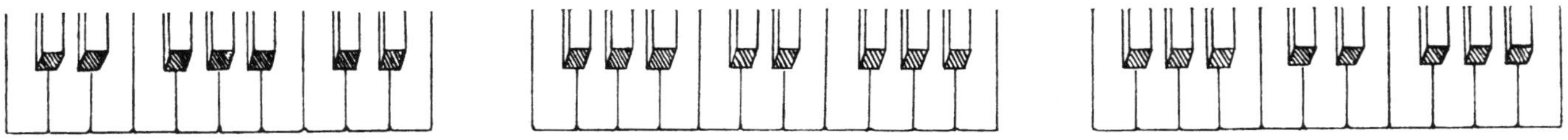

(Write R.H. finger numbers. See chart below.)

Root Position | First Inversion | Second Inversion

(Write letter names.)

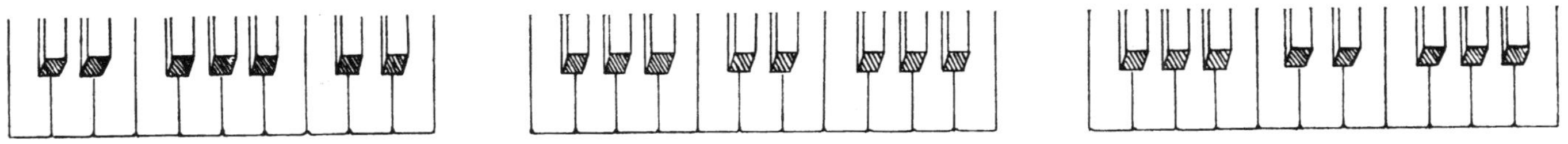

(Write L.H. finger numbers. See chart below.)

KEYBOARD ASSIGNMENT

Right Hand

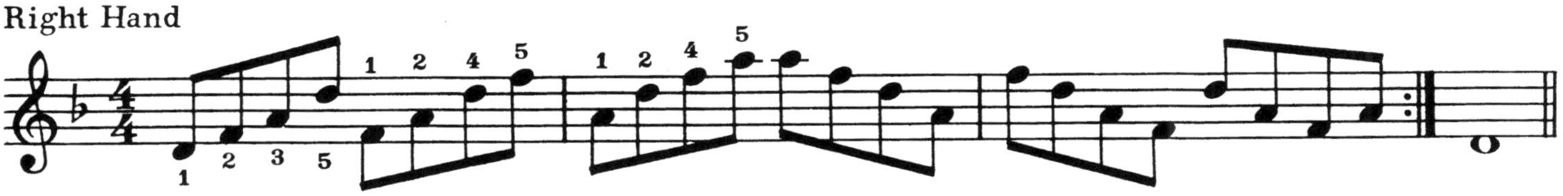

Left Hand

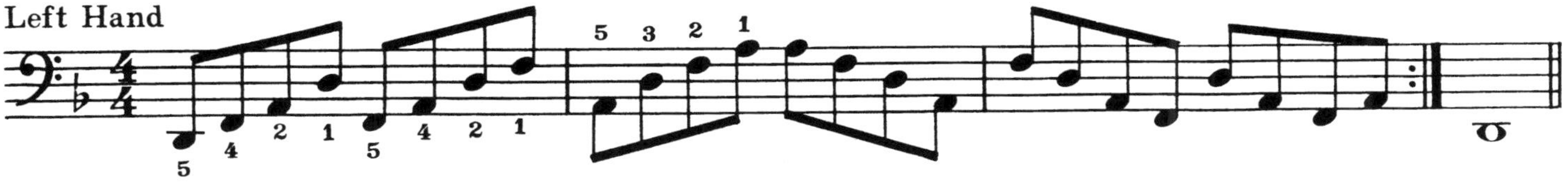

FINGERING AND INVERSION CHART

Left Hand

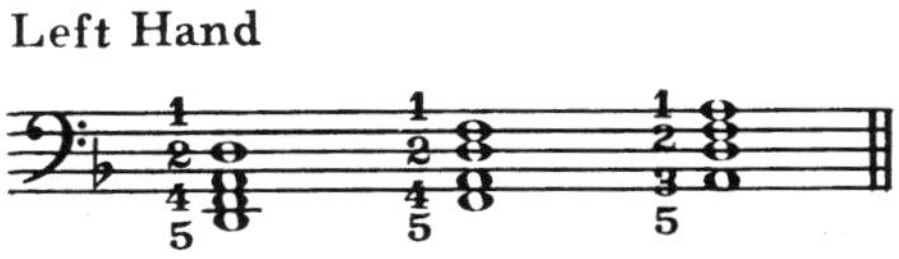

Root Position | First Inversion | Second Inversion

Right Hand

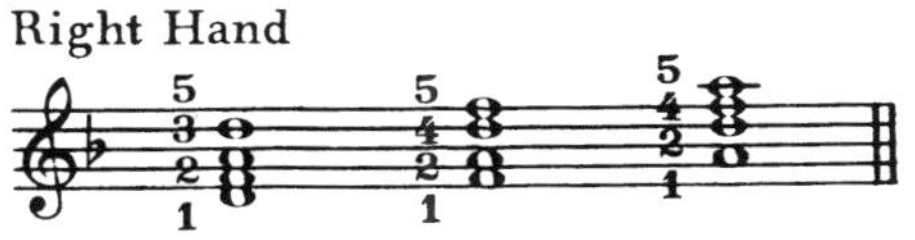

Root Position | First Inversion | Second Inversion

Lesson 23. G Minor Arpeggio

Pupil's Name..

Assignment Date..

Completion Date..

Grade or Star...

DIRECTIONS: On the staffs below, write whole notes for the root position and inversions of the G minor arpeggio. See chart at bottom of page.

Root Position   First Inversion   Second Inversion

(*Write letter names.*)

(*Write R.H. finger numbers. See chart below.*)

Root Position   First Inversion   Second Inversion

(*Write letter names.*)

(*Write L.H. finger numbers. See chart below.*)

KEYBOARD ASSIGNMENT

Right Hand

Left Hand

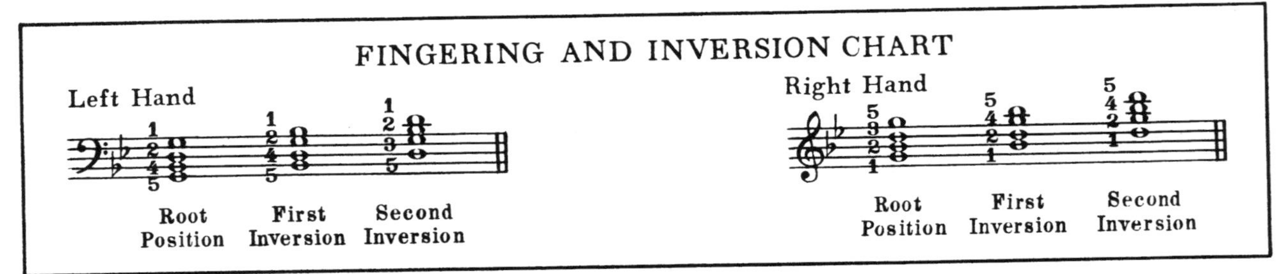

Lesson 24. C Minor Arpeggio

Pupil's Name...

Assignment Date..

Completion Date..

Grade or Star..

DIRECTIONS: On the staffs below, write whole notes for the root position and inversions of the C minor arpeggio. See chart at bottom of page.

Root Position

First Inversion

Second Inversion

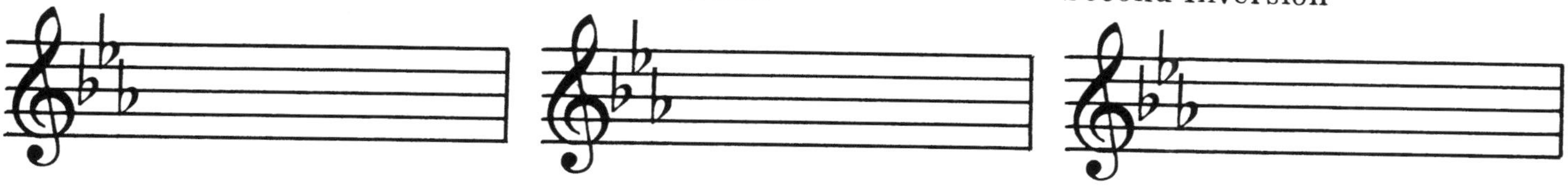

(Write letter names.)

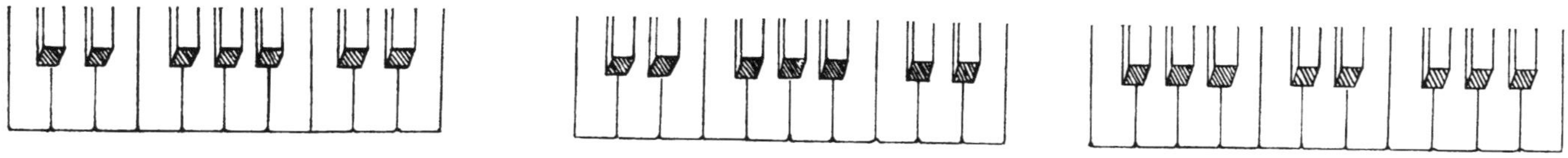

(Write R.H. finger numbers. See chart below.)

Root Position

First Inversion

Second Inversion

(Write letter names.)

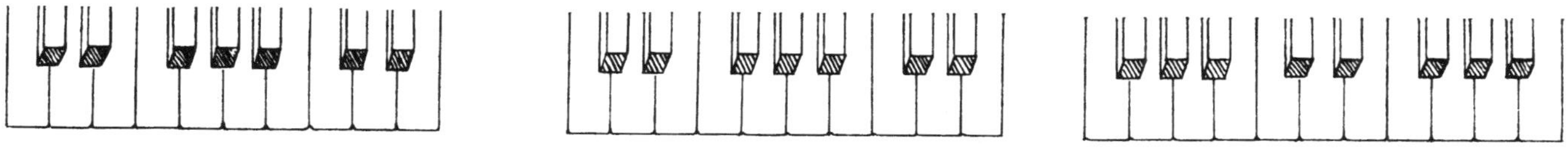

(Write L.H. finger numbers. See chart below.)

KEYBOARD ASSIGNMENT

Right Hand

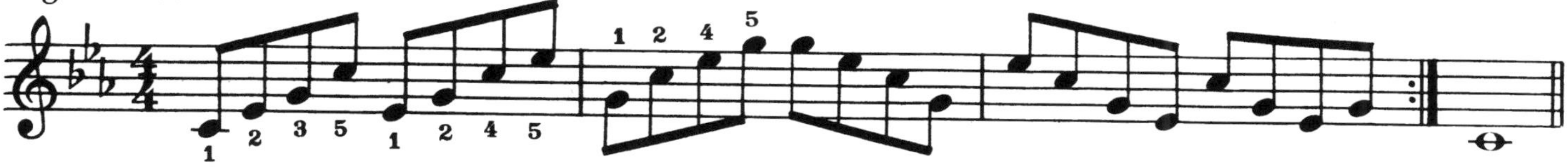

Left Hand

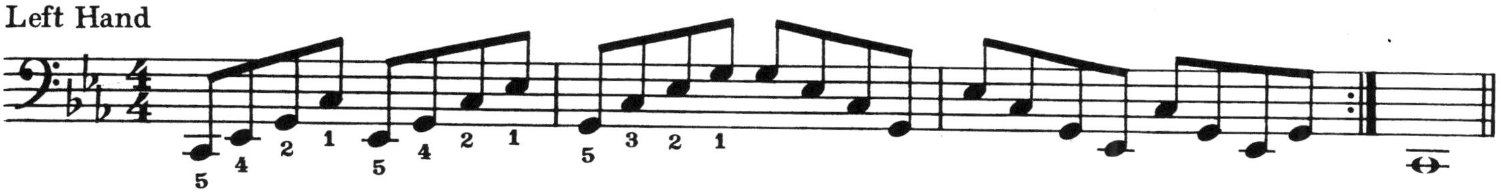

FINGERING AND INVERSION CHART

Left Hand

Root Position	First Inversion	Second Inversion

Right Hand

Root Position	First Inversion	Second Inversion

Lesson 25. F Minor Arpeggio

Pupil's Name...

Completion Date...

Assignment Date...

Grade or Star...

DIRECTIONS: On the staffs below, write whole notes for the root position and inversions of the F minor arpeggio. See chart at bottom of page.

Root Position

First Inversion

Second Inversion

(*Write letter names.*)

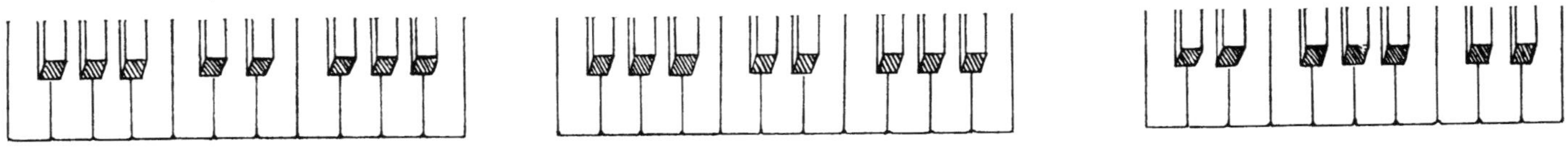

(*Write R.H. finger numbers. See chart below.*)

Root Position

First Inversion

Second Inversion

(*Write letter names.*)

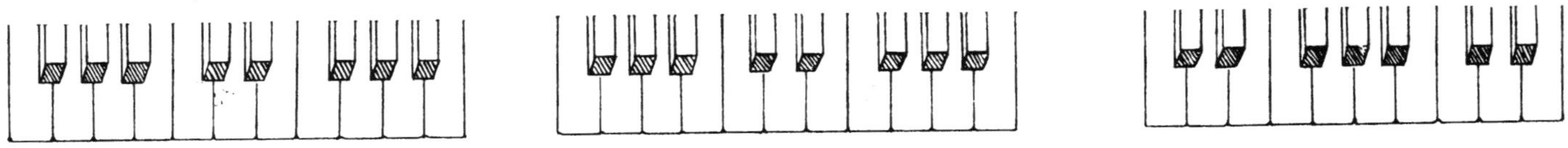

(*Write L.H. finger numbers. See chart below.*)

KEYBOARD ASSIGNMENT

Right Hand

Left Hand

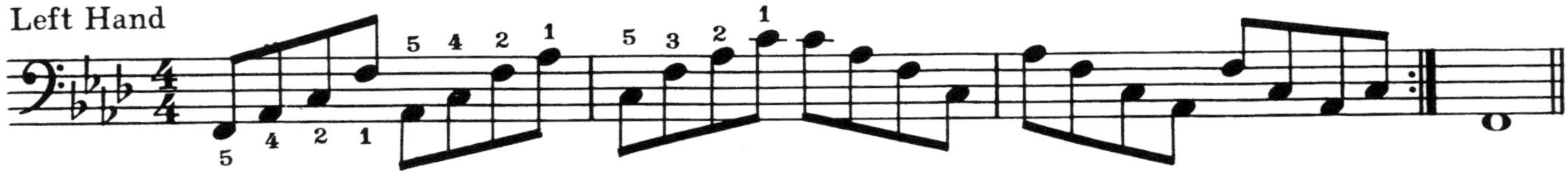

FINGERING AND INVERSION CHART

Left Hand

Right Hand

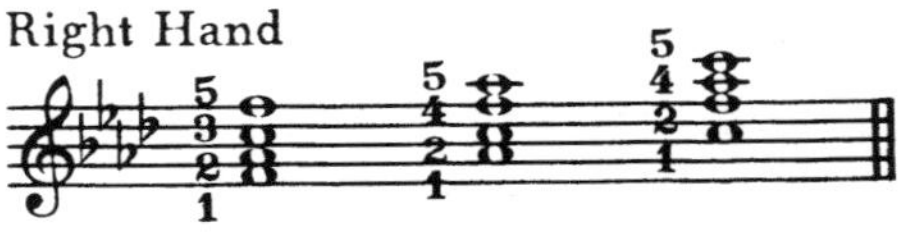

Root Position — First Inversion — Second Inversion

Root Position — First Inversion — Second Inversion

Lesson 26. B Flat Minor Arpeggio

Pupil's Name..

Assignment Date..

Completion Date..

Grade or Star...

DIRECTIONS: On the staffs below, write whole notes for the root position and inversions of the B♭ minor arpeggio. See chart at bottom of page.

Root Position   First Inversion   Second Inversion

(Write letter names.)

(Write R.H. finger numbers. See chart below.)

Root Position   First Inversion   Second Inversion

(Write letter names.)

(Write L.H. finger numbers. See chart below.)

KEYBOARD ASSIGNMENT

Right Hand

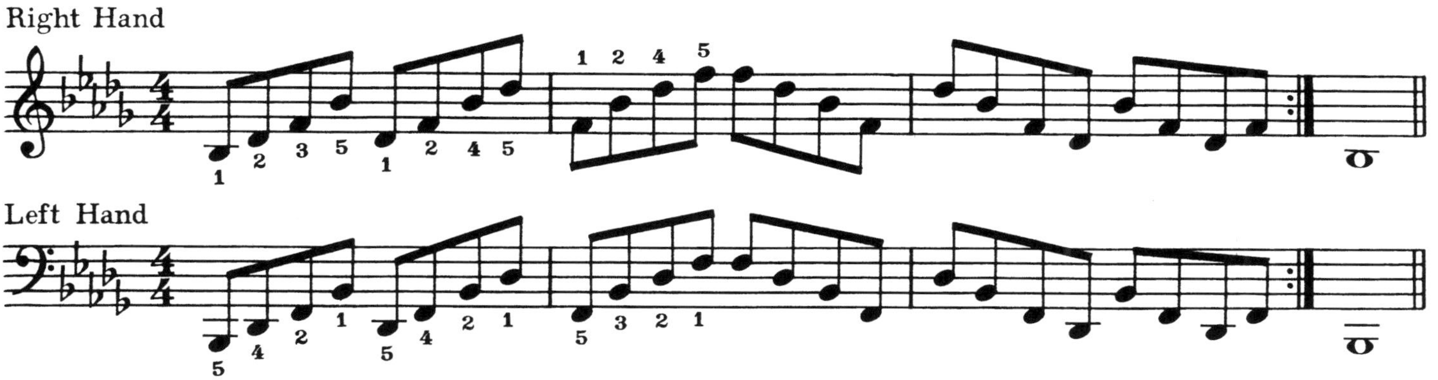

Left Hand

FINGERING AND INVERSION CHART

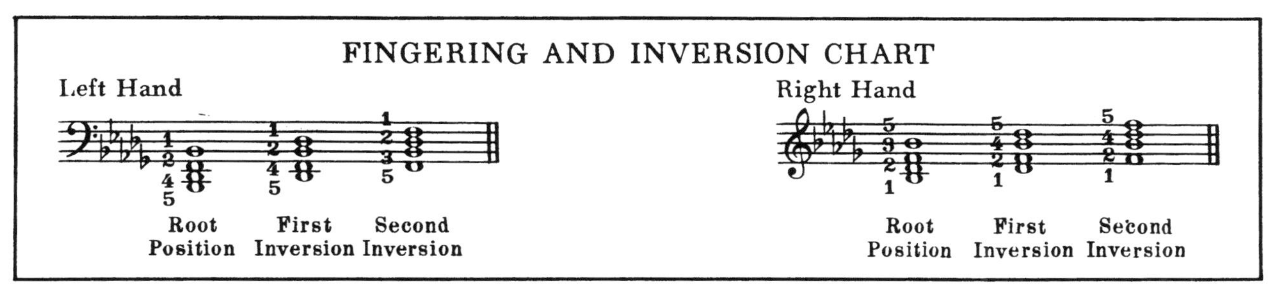

Lesson 27. E Flat Minor Arpeggio

Pupil's Name.. Completion Date..

Assignment Date.. Grade or Star..

DIRECTIONS: On the staffs below, write whole notes for the root position and inversions of the E♭ minor arpeggio. See chart at bottom of page.

Root Position First Inversion Second Inversion

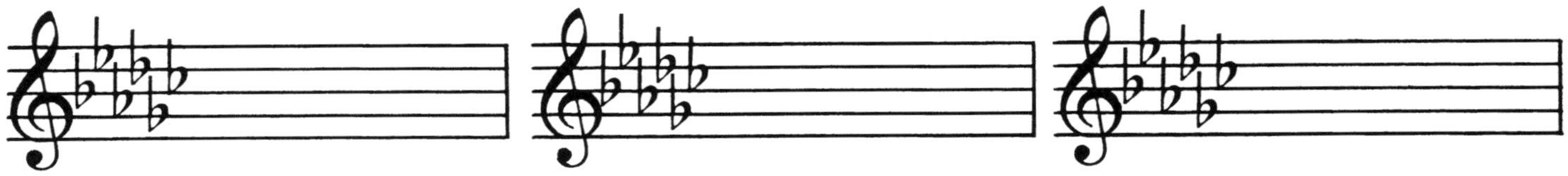

(*Write letter names.*)

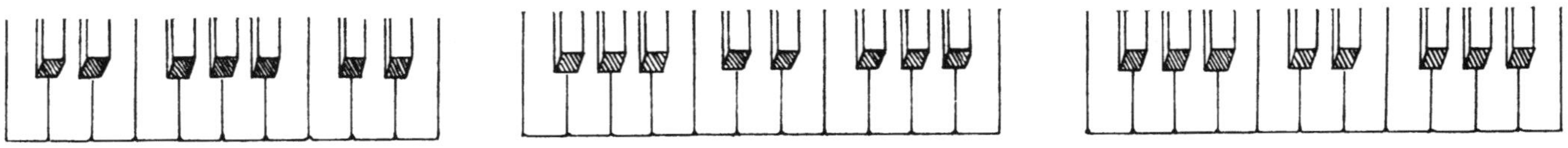

(*Write R.H. finger numbers. See chart below.*)

Root Position First Inversion Second Inversion

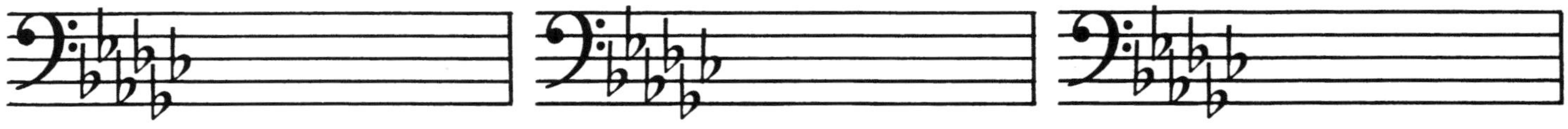

(*Write letter names.*)

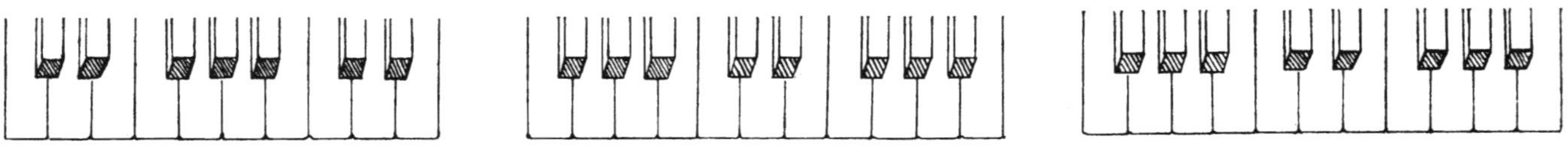

(*Write L.H. finger numbers. See chart below.*)

KEYBOARD ASSIGNMENT

Right Hand

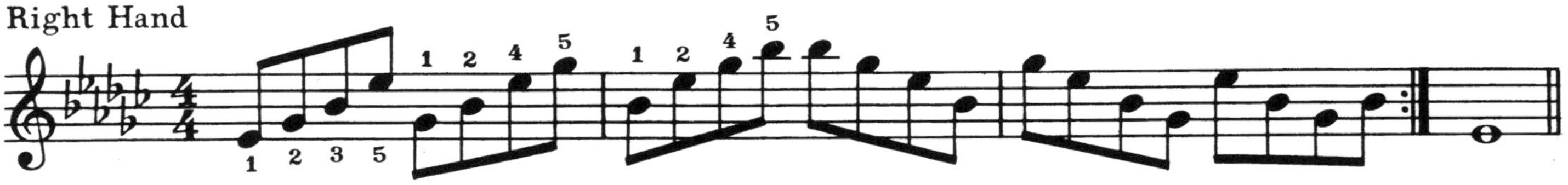

Left Hand

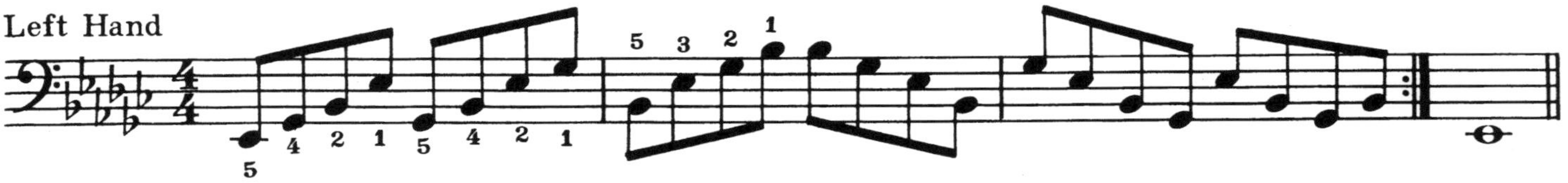

FINGERING AND INVERSION CHART

Left Hand

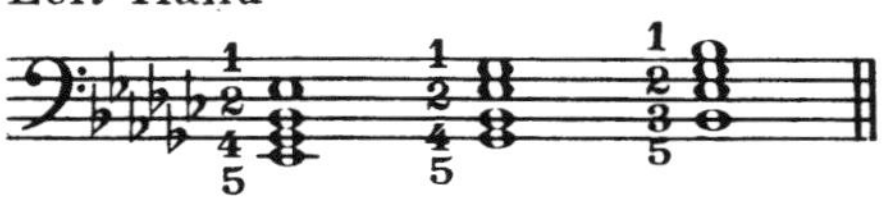

Root Position First Inversion Second Inversion

Right Hand

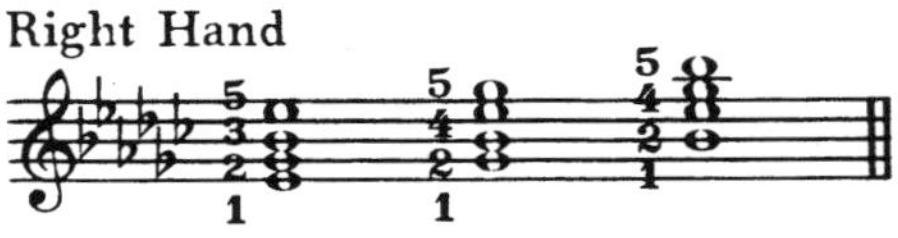

Root Position First Inversion Second Inversion

You are now ready to progress to the Schaum **INTERVAL SPELLER.**

Lesson 28. Arpeggio Quiz No. 4

Pupil's Name..   Completion Date..

Assignment Date..   Grade or Star..

DIRECTIONS: Match each arpeggio at the left with the corresponding chord position at the right by inserting the correct alphabetical letter on the proper dotted line. For example, the answer to No.1 is the "First inversion of B♭ minor," therefore, the letter g has been placed on the dotted line.

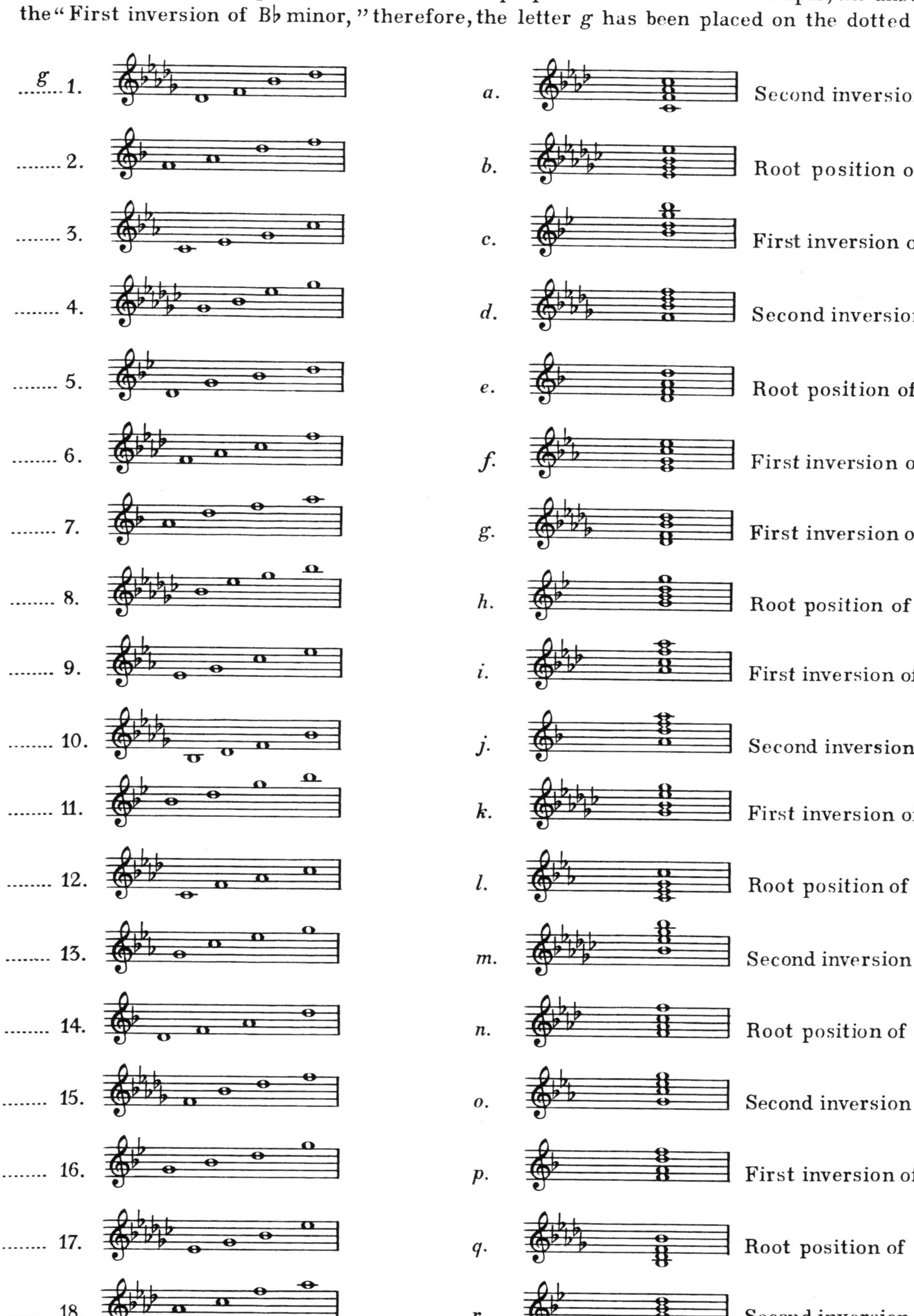